ASIAN AMERICANS
OF ACHIEVEMENT

BRUCE LEE

ASIAN AMERICANS
OF ACHIEVEMENT

ASIAN AMERICANS
OF ACHIEVEMENT

BRUCE LEE

RACHEL A. KOESTLER-GRACK

CHELSEA HOUSE
PUBLISHERS

An imprint of Infobase Publishing

Bruce Lee

Chelsea House
An imprint of Infobase Publishing
132 West 31st Street
New York, NY 10001

ISBN-10: 0-7910-9274-7
ISBN-13: 978-0-7910-9274-3

Library of Congress Cataloging-in-Publication Data
Koestler-Grack, Rachel A., 1973–
  Bruce Lee / Rachel A. Koestler-Grack.
    p. cm. — (Asian Americans of achievement)
  Includes bibliographical references and index.
  ISBN 0-7910-9274-7 (hardcover)
  1. Lee, Bruce, 1940-1973. 2. Actors—United States—Biography. 3. Martial artists—
United States—Biography. I. Title. II. Series.
  PN2287.L2897K64 2007
  791.4302'8092—dc22
  [B]   2006026060

Chelsea House books are available at special discounts when purchased in
bulk quantities for businesses, associations, institutions, or sales promotions.
Please call our Special Sales Department in New York at (212) 967-8800
or (800) 322-8755.

You can find Chelsea House on the World Wide Web at http://www.chelseahouse.com

Text design by Erika K. Arroyo
Cover design by Ben Peterson

Printed in the United States of America

Bang NMSG 10 9 8 7 6 5 4 3 2 1

This book is printed on acid-free paper.

All links and Web addresses were checked and verified to be correct at the time of
publication. Because of the dynamic nature of the Web, some addresses and links may
have changed since publication and may no longer be valid.

CONTENTS

One-Inch Punch

Toward the end of 1963, Bruce Lee stood front and center of the Garfield High School gymnasium in Seattle. In front of him, a couple of dozen scruffy-looking teenagers slouched in their chairs. Garfield was a tough, inner-city school whose students were not strangers to fights. But these kids had never heard of kung fu, the Chinese martial art form Lee was there to demonstrate. A few yawned and checked their wristwatches, and others snickered to each other as they eyed the shrimpy little Asian guy who thought he knew how to fight.

Although kung fu was new to these hoodlums, karate was quite popular in the United States at the time. Lee began by showing them the difference between a karate-style punch and the wing chun centerline punch. The karate punch is delivered from the hip, while a wing chun strike is thrown straight from the solar plexus, or the spot between the naval and the heart, giving a wing chun punch much more force. As he finished speaking, Lee's voice echoed over the muffled whispers of the teens. A moment of silence passed as he peered across his bored audience. He quickly added, "There is a punch with far greater power and can be delivered from a distance of a single inch," according to Bruce Thomas's book, *Bruce Lee: Fighting Spirit*.

Some of the students straightened up in their chairs and cast bewildered glances at each other. An inch—was this guy kidding? Seeing that he'd piqued their curiosity, Lee asked for a volunteer to demonstrate the "one-inch" punch. The group included several husky football and basketball players. Lee looked like he was no match for any number of these boys. While the guys smirked at each other, Bruce pointed to the biggest kid in the bunch and asked him to step forward. The class perked up and even chuckled at how Lee looked like a dwarf next to this burly youth.

Lee pressed his knuckles against the boy's chest and set his balance. "Wait a minute," Lee said and lowered his arm, according to *Fighting Spirit*. He then fumbled through the rows of students, picked up the chair the kid had been sitting in, and set it down about five feet behind his stooge. He resumed his position and said, "Okay, now we're ready." This little theatrical scene heightened the anticipation, and Lee now had the students' full attention.

Realizing Lee meant business, the young brute got a little nervous. He didn't want to get laid out in front of his buddies by a skinny Chinese guy. So he braced himself. Lee's fist was still touching the kid's chest. Suddenly, his arm seemed to make a split-second shimmer. The boy flew off his feet, backward over the chair, and tumbled in somersaults until he lay sprawled out on the floor. Mouths dropped open. No one even saw his arm move.

Stunning crowds was Lee's trademark. The art of kung fu lived and breathed inside of him. It wasn't just a fighting style; it was a way of life. Before Lee came to the United States, kung fu was a well-kept Chinese secret. Kung fu masters lived by a strict code that this martial art should never be taught to Westerners. Lee not only broke that code with his mulitracial students, he

This image of Bruce Lee is from the film *Enter the Dragon* (1973) directed by Robert Clouse. *Enter the Dragon* is an iconic kung fu movie that made Bruce Lee a star. It showcased Lee's unique martial arts style, jeet kune do. Tragically, Bruce Lee died just one month before the movie's release.

was determined to introduce the entire world to kung fu. He defied tradition and put down classical forms, which he thought were unnecessary, inefficient, and impractical in a street fight. Lee asserted that no one should ever waste time with classical moves in a fight. "You'll get clobbered if you do!" he said, according to his wife Linda's *The Bruce Lee Story*.

He continually developed his techniques to be more efficient and effective. Although many people refer to his style as jeet kune do, Lee refused to use the terms "style," "form," or "way" when it came to his fighting system. "Where there is a way, therein lies the limitation," he explained, according to John Little's *Bruce Lee: A Warrior's Journey*. "And when it limits, it traps, and when it traps, it's lifeless, and if it is lifeless, it rots." Lee believed learning was a lifetime process, and he never stopped experimenting with new moves to improve his fighting skills.

Lee's short life was a testament to dedication and unmatched ambition. Upon his return to America, the unruly teen started as a simple waiter. But he quickly gained the reputation of an amazing martial artist. Within years of his arrival, Lee opened his first of three kung fu institutes. Before long, his talents landed him a role on a weekly TV series. He trekked the bitter road to stardom and became a famous actor, his movies smashing all box-office records in Hong Kong. His passion for martial arts made him into the most iconic kung fu fighter the world has ever known.

Little Dragon

On a chilly dawn in November 1940, Grace Li lay alone in a bed at the Jackson Street Hospital in San Francisco's Chinatown. Her husband, Hoi Cheun, a comic actor, was on tour in the United States with the Cantonese Opera Company of Hong Kong. When the company moved on to New York, a very pregnant Grace stayed behind, ready to deliver her baby any day. As the minutes between contractions tightened, no doubt Grace searched the corners of her memory for some shred of her husband's soothing voice. As sunlight peeked over the brick walls of the small Chinese hospital, a new life began. Between 6:00 and 8:00 in the morning of November 27, 1940, Grace gave birth to her third son, who entered the world during the hour of the dragon, in the year of the dragon.

Hoi Cheun and Grace Li felt their children were locked under the unkind eyes of the spirits. Their first child—a boy—died shortly after birth, a bad omen. According to Chinese beliefs, the loss of a son is much worse than the loss of a baby girl. When Grace became pregnant a second time, she feared yet another dark moment. Knowing the second child in a Chinese family should be a girl, the couple adopted a daughter named Phoebe to confuse the spirits. A few months later, Grace gave birth to a healthy boy, Peter. In 1940, a third boy—Grace's second living biological child—was born. Again hoping to fool the spirits, Grace gave the baby a girl's name, Sai Fon (which means "Small Phoenix") and pierced one of his ears. She soon renamed the boy Jun Fan, or "Return Again," because she felt he would one day return to his birthplace. But it was the doctor, Mary Glover, who nicknamed the child "Bruce"—the name that stuck. He later Americanized his family name to Lee.

Five months later, the Lees returned to Hong Kong with their newborn son. The intense heat and humidity carried by the summer monsoon winds soon made him ill, and Bruce spent his early years sickly and weak. Grace constantly doted on her ailing son. But Bruce shook off his toddler frailty and grew into a rambunctious youth. His mother started calling him Mo Si Tung, or "Never Sits Still." "I think I spoiled him because he was so sick," Grace later said in M. Uyehara's *Bruce Lee: Incomparable Fighter*. "As he grew older, he got better . . . he was sometimes too active for me." During his childhood, if Bruce sat still for even a moment, his family thought something was terribly wrong with the boy. The only time he stopped jumping, running, fidgeting, and babbling was when he disappeared in a quiet corner curled up with a book. He sometimes stayed up half the night reading. In fact, Grace believed his long hours of reading caused him to become nearsighted at age six, when he needed to wear glasses.

Bruce grew up in Kowloon City at 218 Nathan Road, in a two-bedroom flat on the second floor of an old building. The narrow stairway that led up to the Lees' apartment had no door at the street level, and homeless passersby often camped out in the entrance. But two sets of bulky doors on the second-floor landing separated Bruce's home from the street dwellers, the outer doors lavished with steel bars, the inner doors dotted with peepholes.

Bruce Lee was born in San Francisco, California, in 1940. When he was just one year old, his parents returned with their newborn son to Kowloon, Hong Kong. Shown above is a sprawling image of Lee's hometown, circa 1955. Bruce was known to get into fights with schoolyard gangs during his tumultuous years growing up in Kowloon.

Inside the flat, rooms were open and scarce of furniture. The larger main room had a refrigerator at one end and served as a living room, dining room, and bedroom. Throughout the day, the family gathered around the large table to eat, talk, read, and play. At night, the children sprawled in iron-frame beds, not needing to cover up with blankets in the relentless heat. From the dining area branched two smaller rooms. One housed two bunk beds, and the other opened to a veranda that overlooked Nathan Road. During summer, the veranda was piled with potted plants, and, at one time, a caged chicken.

When Hoi Cheun's brother died, his widow and their five children came to live with the Lee family, as is Chinese custom. Together with a couple of servants and Wu Ngan—an unofficially adopted child—as many as 20 people sometimes crammed into the flat. This is not to mention the dogs, birds, and fish. Bruce's favorite dog was an Alsatian named Bobby, who slept under his bed every night.

Despite the crowded and sometimes chaotic household, the Lees were far from underprivileged. In addition to his opera

BRUCE LEE'S HONG KONG

Today, planes glide over the rooftops of Kowloon City and swoop down into Hong Kong's Kai Tak airport for some of the trickiest landings in the world, onto a narrow runway that juts out into the busy harbor. Ferries, jetfoils, and junks dot the waters below, and, as the planes descend, tiny sampans captained by women in straw hats can be seen cutting the wakes of broader vessels. Along the water's edge rise skyscrapers and luxury hotels of steel and glass, the windows and harbor surface playing a game of Ping-Pong with beams of sunshine. The streets beyond are a mess of tangled traffic, car horns, and construction racket. Beyond the flawless skyscrapers, the Porsches and Mercedes, the businessmen who live like sultans, lies an area of town almost untouched by time, a place very similar to the world of young Bruce Lee.

Before Bruce was born, Hong Kong, including Kowloon City and the lands known as the New Territories, were ruled as British colonies. When Bruce was just a toddler, Hong Kong entered a dark age during the Japanese occupation of World War II. Many people were executed by the Japanese army during the wartime occupation, which lasted three years and eight months, returning income, Hoi Cheun received payments from rental properties. Therefore, the Lees could always afford servants to help with the extra work. However, Bruce seemed to be only mildly impressed with his father's lifestyle. In Chinese culture, the relationship between father and son is often distanced, and Hoi Cheun wasn't home enough to make a strong impression on the young mind of his son. Bruce sometimes complained about his "miserly" father and how Hoi Cheun had at times stolen money to take friends out to eat. He also smoked opium from time to time, and, at one point, according to Bruce Thomas's *Bruce Lee: Fighting Spirit*, admitted, "I smoke opium because it helps sweeten my singing voice." But Hoi Cheun didn't tuck all his money away. He was

to British control in 1945. The port once again opened but was suddenly overrun in 1949 with masses of Chinese refugees fleeing the civil war and the new Communist government in China.

Thousands of Chinese people moved into the city. With nowhere to go, many of them made their homes on the streets, in doorways and stairwells, and on rooftops, or they built shanties in the park or in rundown areas of town. Everyday life exploded into a fierce struggle. Gangs popped up as a means of crude survival. Restless youths wandered the streets, looking for excitement and perhaps a little cash. In dark corners of town, the gangs rumbled in fistfights and bloody knife battles. Even years later, actor Jim Kelly was surprised at the rough-and-tough teenage gangs. "I thought the teenage gangs in the U.S. were tough," he commented in Linda Lee's *The Bruce Lee Story*, "but they're real tame compared to those in Hong Kong. The gangs . . . are vicious."

Bruce Lee's Hong Kong was a daily fight for respect and strength. One moment's falter could mean falling to the underdog, becoming the weak. In a city rabid with violence and running with wild gangs, weakness was the most dreaded trait.

known to gamble and sometimes paid medical bills for friends who couldn't afford them.

With his father away and too many people at home, Bruce spent much of his childhood amusing himself on the streets of Hong Kong. The maze of roadways below the Lees' second-floor flat wound between ramshackle apartment buildings and bustling shops and restaurants. Local vendors wearing long shirts or black pajama-like suits stood in front of canopied carts stacked with fruits and vegetables, fish and duck. A blend of exotic aromas hung in the thick, muggy air. The narrow roads that Bruce wandered as a child were littered with rubbish and a smattering of rotting foods, but they were much more exciting to him than school classrooms.

In a busy household like the Lees' one child is not often missed, but Grace often had to deal with the trouble Bruce caused. Although the Lees paid school fees every month, Bruce's mother got frequent calls from teachers wondering why he missed classes. Grace begged Bruce to go to school, rattling pitches about how important it was, how he needed a good education to make it in the world. Still, Bruce just couldn't get his feet to carry him to class. Even though he showed a mild interest in history and social studies, he detested math and sciences. As his mother later joked in Linda Lee's *The Bruce Lee Story*, "By the time he was ten, that was as far as he could count." Finally, Grace told him it didn't matter so much if he didn't like school, but he had to at least tell her where he was going to play so she would always know where to find him.

While Bruce played hooky from school, he dreamt up practical jokes to experiment on friends and family. He started with simple gags, like "electric shock" tricks and itching powder. Oftentimes, he could barely hold down his laughter long enough to deliver the "punch line." But his jokes quickly became more elaborate. On one occasion, he rearranged the furniture in the apartment to confuse the cleaning maid. He once coaxed his brother Robert to pretend he was a submarine and look up his coat sleeve like it was a periscope. As Robert peered into the dark sleeve, Bruce poured water down the other side, splashing Robert in the face. Other pranks turned out to be less funny. After pushing his sister Phoebe into the swimming pool, she caught him and dunked his head under the water until he promised to never do it again. From that day on, Bruce refused to go into a swimming pool.

Despite Bruce's rebellious tendencies, at times he had an extremely kind heart. Grace remembered one day when Bruce sat focused on something happening on the street below. Suddenly, he darted out the door. When Grace looked out the window, she saw Bruce helping a blind man across the street. Later, he told her that he just had to help the poor man, who looked so sad and frustrated by the people ignoring him as they walked by.

Still, there were times Grace worried about the future of her troublemaker child. "Bruce never changed his character," she said, according to *Fighting Spirit*. "He repeated the same mistakes time after time. I was disappointed with him again and again. Once I asked how he expected to earn his living if he kept on like that. He said, 'I'll become a famous film star one day.'" She scolded him and told him the life of a movie star was not as grand as it seemed. "You can't even behave as a normal person," she argued. "How do you expect to become a famous film star?" But Bruce was already on his way to the silver screen. Deep inside, he knew he was special and was going to make something great of his life.

A RISING YOUNG STAR

Few actors have started a major film career as young as Bruce Lee did. He was barely three months old when he played a part in a Chinese movie made in San Francisco called *Golden Gate Girl*. In the film, he played a female baby, carried by his father. In this first movie he was more or less a stage prop, so Bruce considered his first professional screen debut to be his role in *The Beginning of a Boy*, which he made in Hong Kong when he was six years old. He played a street kid who fights with a shoeshine boy, who was played by a good friend of his named Unicorn.

Also at age six, Bruce starred in his first role under the name Lee Siu Lung, or Lee Little Dragon, the name by which he would become known in Hong Kong and Southeast Asia; he appeared with his father in this movie, titled *My Son, Ah Cheun*. Bruce had a more important role in this film, cast as the cute costar to the top Cantonese film comic Chow Shui. He played the part of a streetwise kid trying to survive a life in Hong Kong sweatshops. In both tragedies and comedies like *It's Father's Fault*, Bruce's early roles were of street urchins and orphans.

Being an actor at such a young age can be overwhelmingly hard work. But Bruce never seemed to mind the long hours on the set. Whenever he had to work late at night or get up before sunrise, he rarely complained. "He liked it very much," Grace later recalled in *The Bruce Lee Story*. "At two o'clock in the morning, I'd call out, 'Bruce, the car is here,' and he'd leap up and put on his shoes and go off very cheerfully. There was no trouble getting him up when it came to making a film." She lightly added, "When I had to get him up for school in the mornings, however, it was quite a different story."

Having a father as an actor helped Bruce get early exposure to the world of acting. Hoi Cheun sometimes took his son to the opera. It was at these shows that Bruce met the son of another actor in the Chinese opera, Siu Kee Lun, better known to his friends as Unicorn. Although he was three years older than Bruce, the two boys quickly became close friends. In the neighborhood streets, they would fight and fence with bamboo swords. Bruce imitated Robin Hood, the hero of one of his favorite films. Even though Unicorn was older and stronger, Bruce never admitted defeat. He would continue battling until Unicorn finally got tired and gave up.

Although Bruce was often in trouble with his father for fighting, his street-smart toughness no doubt helped his film career. In his later films, he played juvenile delinquents and teenage rebels. Even in his early fight scenes, Bruce was already using some gestures that would one day become his trademarks: the admonishing finger, a thumb wiped across the nose, the brushing down of his jacket sleeves, and his steady, burning gaze. As a child actor, Bruce appeared in 20 pictures. The best-known movie of his early years was *The Orphan*, a film about Hong Kong street gangs. Made when he was 18, this picture featured his only leading role.

Throughout his teenage years, Bruce not only collected stage experience from pretend play fights and opera seats. He knew firsthand the heat of a street fight. His membership in a Chinese street gang, and the films he watched growing up, prepared Bruce for a whole new world both on and off the screen.

PUNK OF THE STREETS

After attending Chinese elementary schools, however infrequently, Bruce started at La Salle College, a Catholic boys' school, at age 12. Teachers taught classes in English, even though most of the boys were Chinese and had no English-speaking history, as was the case with Bruce. Although constantly in trouble from the first day, he managed to attract the attention of one of the better teachers, Brother Henry Pang. Many of the teachers found Bruce stubborn, lazy, or wild, but the round-faced Brother Henry saw a bright youngster full of potential. He recognized that Bruce just needed a different teaching approach. Brother Henry channeled Bruce's restlessness into helpful activities—running errands, erasing blackboards, and opening windows. Although Bruce willingly performed the tasks, he still found it impossible to sit still during class, and his continual disturbances got him labeled as a troublemaker.

Back in the 1940s, the British Crown Colony of Hong Kong, including the city of Kowloon and its suburbs in the New Territories, was a crowded, restless place where people struggled fiercely to survive. Bruce spent his childhood there during the Japanese occupation of World War II. Once, he stood on the veranda over Nathan Road and shook his fist defiantly in the air at a Japanese plane flying overhead. In the years following the 1949 Communist triumph over mainland China, ten-year-old Bruce heard

The Royal Leicestershire Regiment travels on a Kowloon street heading toward their barracks on June 14, 1949. British forces once occupied Hong Kong. The troops were there to bolster support in case of a threat from Communist China.

many stories of frightened refugees coming to the colony, fleeing famine and oppression in China. Gangs of young Chinese boys roamed the streets of Kowloon, looking for adventure and any chance to unleash some pent-up anger and frustration.

The Chinese hated the British almost as much as they despised the Japanese. "Kids there have nothing to look forward to," Bruce later explained, as retold in *The Bruce Lee Story*. "The white kids (British) have all the best jobs and the rest of us had to work for them. That's why most of the kids become punks."

The Chinese students of Bruce's school felt an intense rivalry with the British schoolchildren of King George V School up the hill from La Salle College. Bruce became the leader of a gang that hung out after school behind the playing field fence of King George V. The boys would gather on the hill and shout taunts at the British school kids, which culminated in some fierce fist-fights. The rumbles would continue until one side was obviously beaten or the police broke it up.

Soon, phone calls and nightly visits by the police became a regular occurrence at the Lee house. When Hoi Cheun came home late from the theater, Bruce would hide under the covers and pretend to be asleep to avoid punishment. Oftentimes, Grace simply "forgot" to tell her husband about the day's events. There were times, however, when Grace could not hide her son's unruly behavior. If Bruce came home with a black eye or some other visible injury, Hoi Cheun flew into a rage, placing all sorts of restrictions on Bruce. But he was not home enough to enforce any of his punishments, and they had little effect on the Little Dragon.

As Bruce and his gang continued to spar with the King George students, the young punk began thinking more and more about his actual strength and fighting techniques. Being somewhat of a scrawny youth, Bruce recalled in M. Uyehara's *Bruce Lee: Incomparable Fighter*, "I always fought with my gang behind me. In school, our favorite weapon was the chains we'd find in the cans (bathroom toilets). Those days, kids improvised all kinds of weapons—even shoes with razors attached." In the 1950s, Hong Kong was a city of desperation, where one gang preyed on another just to survive. Bruce began wondering what would happen to him if his gang wasn't around to back him up. Would he be able to protect himself from a rival gang? He decided not to take any chances. He was determined to be trained in the most effective style of martial arts at the time: kung fu.

Fighting Crazy

Although Bruce Lee was part of a wealthy family and had the opportunity to attend fine private schools, he was drawn to the rough and ragged crowds of the streets. He eventually formed his own street gang, the Tigers of Junction Street. From time to time, Bruce and the Tigers finished on the losing side of a fight. Bruised and bleeding, Bruce would storm home, demanding to be trained in martial arts so he could defend himself. Eventually, his father showed him some t'ai chi, but the slow-flowing movements of this type of martial art offered little help in a street fight. T'ai chi is closer to a therapeutic art that has more mental value than physical. Besides, it takes decades of practice before t'ai chi can be used as an effective fighting tool, and Bruce had no patience for that.

Still, Bruce sometimes went with his father to t'ai chi lessons. "I got tired of it quickly," Bruce later confessed in M. Uyehara's *Bruce Lee: Incomparable Fighter*. "It was no fun for a kid. Just a bunch of old men." On one occasion, he hurt a t'ai chi instructor on purpose. He was 15 at the time and had already started training in another martial arts form. The teacher often put on demonstrations to prove his strength, calling up volunteers to punch him in the stomach. One after another, members of the audience tried to hurt the old man but failed. Finally, Bruce raised his hand and went up. The old man smiled and exposed his stomach. As hard as he could, Bruce deliberately thrust his right hand into the instructor's ribs. There was a quick crack, and the man crumbled to the floor moaning. Obviously unimpressed by t'ai chi, Bruce went searching for a fighting form that would prove useful.

Many neighborhood gangs had ties to a local kung fu school. One of the students was William Cheung, a well-known street fighter. Bruce had first met William many years earlier, when William's uncle—who had friends in the Chinese Opera—invited him to Bruce's birthday party. William practiced a formidable style of kung fu known as wing chun. In his hour of need, Bruce sought out William and pestered him day after day to teach him the style. At first, William didn't take Bruce—an actor who moonlighted with a so-called gang—seriously. "The Tigers were just eight people who got together, they weren't all that tough," William Cheung recalled years later in Bruce Thomas's *Bruce Lee: Fighting Spirit*. "They got their fur singed a lot. I told Bruce that because he was a film actor, he shouldn't fight but look after his appearance." But when Bruce showed up with a handful of money for lessons, William finally took Bruce to his kung fu school at Restaurant Workers Union Hall. There, he introduced Bruce to the master, Yip Man. Because Bruce was somewhat of a celebrity, Yip Man was eager to take him and began teaching him on the spot.

Thirteen-year-old Bruce took to wing chun with enthusiasm that quickly turned into obsession. Yip Man's son, Yip Chun, described him as "fighting crazy." At first, the teenager was only interested in what he could use for street fighting. But as the lessons continued, Yip Man introduced him to the finer points of the art—meditation, breathing, and balance. No doubt, these early years of martial arts training were crucial building blocks to the personal fighting method and philosophy Bruce would eventually develop.

KUNG FU

Originally, kung fu—or as Bruce like to call it, gung fu—was not the name of any style of martial art. Rather it was a term that meant "the accomplishment of a difficult task" or "hard work and time spent," according to *Fighting Spirit*. Today, kung fu has become a general description for many of the Chinese martial arts.

According to martial art folklore, the father of kung fu was an early-sixteenth-century Indian monk named Bodhidharma, who left his monastery in India to spread the teachings of Buddha in China. As he wandered through the mountains of northern China, he stopped at a Shaolin monastery ("Shaolin" in Mandarin; "Sil Lum" in Cantonese). *Shaolin* means "young tree," or a tree that can survive wild storms and strong winds because it is flexible and can bend and sway. Bodhidharma was not welcomed at this monastery because his thoughts on Buddhism differed from the monks' beliefs. Instead, Bodhidharma found refuge in a nearby cave where he lived for the next nine years, spending long hours in meditation. Finally, the 70-year-old hermit returned to Shaolin. His years of reclusion and meditation had given him a strong presence of authority and knowledge. This time, the monks did not question him.

An aged Bodhidharma began teaching the Shaolin monks how to meditate. Much to his displeasure, he found that the monks constantly fell asleep during meditation. He decided this happened because the monks spent so much mental energy on their other studies during the day that their bodies became stressed and weak. He created a series of exercises to help the Shaolin monks grow stronger. "Although the way of the Buddha is preached for the soul, the body and soul are inseparable," he explained. "For this reason, I shall give you a method by which

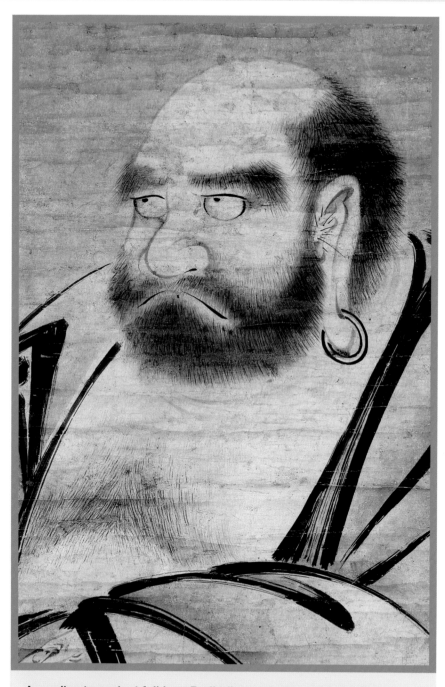

According to ancient folklore, Bodhidharma is the original father of kung fu and the founder of Zen Buddhism. Portraits of Bodhidharma (*above*) reveal his Indian heritage by emphasizing his dark features.

you can develop your energy enough to attain to the essence of the Buddha."

His exercises were actually a series of fighting moves as a form of active meditation. These movements became the basis of Shaolin boxing and the root of many kung fu styles. The training served a dual purpose, also allowing the monks to defend themselves against bandits when traveling between monasteries. However, Bodhidharma's main focus was not merely on building physical strength or fighting techniques, but on developing and nurturing the intrinsic energy of ch'i—translated as "breath," "spirit," or "life-force."

Ch'i is energy that fuels the entire universe and encompasses the vital energy of every living thing. In the human body, ch'i consists of the energy that flows from breathing and the heartbeat, as well as the working muscles and nervous system. In other words, ch'i is all physical, mental, and emotional activity. Most Western doctors separate these functions into circulatory, digestive, muscular, and endocrine systems, but the Chinese view the body systems in unity. The development of ch'i creates the base of all Taoist arts.

In 1768, the Manchu dynasty destroyed the Shaolin temple and conquered the then-ruling Ming dynasty. Still today, the traditional kung fu greeting is to fold an open hand over a clenched fist, symbolizing the Sun and Moon, whose characters in Chinese mean "Ming." This action shows respect for the Ming dynasty, whose fall started with the destruction of the temple. Only five people, called the Venerable Five, escaped Shaolin. Of these, Ng Mui was the only female member of the monastery to survive. She went into hiding but continued to practice kung fu.

About this time, a breathtaking young woman named Yim Wing Chun (Everlasting Springtime) became engaged to a man who lived in a distant land. At the same time, Wing Chun's beauty also attracted the attention of a local gangster. Day after day, he harassed her to break off the engagement and marry him instead. Still in hiding, Ng Mui heard about the rogue's threats. She came to Yim Wing Chun with a plan to rid herself of the nuisance gangster.

First, she instructed Wing Chun's father to write a letter to her fiancé breaking off the engagement. At the same time, he was to tell the gangster that because of the great distance the letter had to travel, the new wedding should be postponed for a year. This move bought the two women some time. At once, Ng Mui began training Wing Chun to fight. As the weeks rolled by, Wing Chun realized that a year would never be long enough to learn all the techniques Ng Mui was teaching her. After all, Shaolin had 38 forms, or practice routines, that Wing Chun was trying to master. Therefore, she stripped down the teachings to their most effective basics. She condensed them into three phases—the *sil um tao* (little idea), *chum kil* (searching for the opening), and the deadly *bil jee* (stabbing fingers). She spent the remainder of the year perfecting these forms.

At the end of the year, Wing Chun's father told the gangster that his daughter would only marry someone who could defeat her in hand-to-hand combat. Priding himself as a pretty good fighter, the would-be groom accepted her challenge. He quickly discovered that his classic blocking and punching was of no use against the simple and direct fighting of Wing Chun.

And so the style passed down through six generations to Yip Man, who began learning the art at age 13 but didn't start teaching it until he was 56. Two years later, young Bruce Lee walked into his classroom with a fist of crumpled bills and a stubborn expression. Yip Man did not have the appearance of a typical fighter. He was quiet-mannered and small-framed, standing only five and a half feet tall. Yet his presence was imposing and his beliefs staunch. He despised Western clothing, refused to pose for publicity photographs, and insisted that only the Chinese should be taught wing chun.

SERIOUS WING CHUN STUDENT

Immediately, Bruce took to the wing chun style of fighting. He was attracted to its emphasis on developing energy and the way it delivered "the maximum of anguish with the minimum of movement." The foundation of this particular style rests on the principle that the shortest distance between two points is a straight line. Bruce found that wing chun did not have any big circular movements like his father's t'ai chi. Even though he learned kicks, none of them struck higher than the opponent's waist. The object was to fight as close to the enemy as possible. All attacks were aimed at the central axis of the opponent's body. In the same way, Bruce learned to protect his own axis.

The effectiveness of wing chun is dependent on the technique of chi sao, or "sticking hands." Chi sao is not an actual fighting move but rather a practice that develops an acute awareness to the shifting balance of physical forces during a fight. When two people fight, there is a point of contact. In time at this point, a chi sao student would be able to feel any move or intended move. This response is called a contact reflex. For example, this reflex is similar to the sensation a fisherman gets when there is a bite on his line. He doesn't have to actually see a fish nibbling the bait to know the fish is there. With experience, the contact reflex can be so refined that the fighter can block any attack and counter instantly and automatically.

Chi sao has three stages of training. Bruce started by blocking and countering predetermined moves. He then progressed to random moves, until eventually he trained while blindfolded. Although the practice routines of chi sao may not apply to a real fight, the coordination and awareness they polish are crucial. Through chi sao training, Bruce gained his first practical experience of the energies yin and yang—the yielding and active forces of the universe.

During chi sao training, Bruce applied the same principles of yin and yang—pressure and release—while trying to "feel" the force and intention of his opponent's attacks so he could stop or counter the moves. His hands and arms were constantly moving between precise positions, but he always had to be alert and respond to a shifting balance of forces. He learned to keep his body ready for small changes during a fight, holding his arms loose but not limp, understanding that the arms still must be firm and strong enough to stand up to punches and pressure without being rigid. Ultimately, the one who can spontaneously adapt to the changing movements and forces will win the fight. If Bruce learned to find the gaps in his opponent's defensive moves, he could counter blows quickly, naturally, and effectively. With much practice, this skill would become reflex and make him a deadly contender. Wing Chun would teach him how to "feel" his opponent—sense his attacker's next move and stop it before it was even delivered.

Another training exercise of wing chun is practice fighting with a wooden dummy that represents the opponent. The routine breaks down almost all conceivable combat situations into 108 practice moves. In addition, fighting against a surface of solid wood toughens and conditions the hands into unbreakable weapons that can deliver a bricklike blow to the enemy.

Like most students, Bruce started learning kung fu because of its excellent reputation compared to other fighting methods. But many of the first forms were dull and monotonous. Bruce became frustrated and impatient, according to *Fighting Spirit*. Everyone wanted to speed through the early stages so they could start sticking hands. But the single sticking hands wasn't much fun either. When he finally got to the double, he thought, "I can fight now!" If he could land a punch, he felt a surge of pride. Egos ran hot among the students. Everyone wanted to beat his partner and become top dog.

Yip Man told Bruce to relax and not get so excited. But it was hard to stay calm during a fight. When someone struck him, Bruce quickly became angry and wanted to strike back. Bruce watched Yip Man stick hands with the other students.

He noticed how relaxed Yip Man was. Sometimes, he threw his partner out without even having to hit him. When Bruce did sticking hands with Yip Man, he felt his balance being controlled by the teacher. He was always off balance, with his toes or heels off the ground. When he tried to strike, his hands rebounded off Yip Man, as if Bruce's own force was being used against him. Yet the old man's moves were so slight and without violence. When students asked how he did it, Yip Man demonstrated the practice forms they had hated to learn. Bruce quickly realized the importance of patience in learning kung fu.

While training, Bruce was not only trying to master the physical techniques, but also he was learning to quell the interference of emotions such as fear and anger. He found it hard to move slowly. He wanted to learn how to *fight*. But Yip Man explained that good and bad techniques are rooted in good or bad body forms, and he suggested Bruce quit sticking hands for a while. Despite his rash desires, a true understanding of the art sprouted in him. Much to his own surprise, he took Yip Man's advice and stopped sticking hands. Instead, he spent long hours in contemplation. He walked along the harbor, far away from the noises of the city. Why was form so important? he wondered. What did it have to do with what was happening around him? After about four years of kung fu training, Bruce finally began to feel the principle of gentleness in the art, the quiet way of neutralizing an opponent's moves while using as little energy as possible. "It sounded simple," Bruce admitted, according to *Bruce Lee: The Celebrated Life of the Golden Dragon*, "but in actual application it was difficult."

Every day after school, Bruce hurried straight to Yip Man's class, only stopping from time to time to practice his kicks on a tree. Even later at home during dinner, he would punch the chair next to him—always trying to improve his moves. Before long, some of the older, more advanced students complained to William Cheung about the way Bruce beat them during training fights. "They were upset because he was progressing so fast,"

Dragon: The Bruce Lee Story is a fictionalized biographical account of Bruce Lee's life starting from his young rambunctious days in Hong Kong, to his well-earned stardom in the United States. The film shows Bruce Lee learning martial arts at a young age.

Cheung recalled in *Fighting Spirit*. "I noticed that, even when he was talking, he was always doing some kind of arm or leg movement. That's when I realized he was actually serious about kung fu."

Jealous students at the wing chun class wanted Bruce gone. He was making them look bad. Somehow, they found out that Bruce had German ancestors. Knowing that Yip Man only taught the Chinese, they pressured him to stop teaching Bruce. But Yip Man genuinely like Bruce and his raw enthusiasm for the art and refused to expel him. Soon, students threatened to leave the school, so Bruce quit of his own will.

For a time, he continued training with one of Yip Man's senior pupils, Wong Sheung Leung, who had his own group of students. To get personal instruction, Bruce sometimes headed off Wong's students on their way to class and told them the teacher was sick. Later, he began training every weekend with William Cheung instead. Even William Cheung was impressed with this young man's fiery passion to become the best.

CHA-CHA CHAMP

By the time Bruce was 15, he was quite popular among the neighborhood kids in Kowloon. It wasn't long before he started attracting the attention of the ladies as well. A year after he began kung fu classes, Bruce also took up dancing the cha-cha, probably because he had a crush on his partner, Pearl Cho. Not only did dancing gain the attention of his love interest, it also helped develop his balance and footwork for kung fu. Like other areas of interest, Bruce wanted to be the best in dance. He carried a card in his wallet on which he had listed more than 100 dance steps. And he practiced his suave moves almost every night of the week at the Champagne night club at Tsimshatsui.

Each evening, Bruce ironed his shirt and slacks. Before leaving the apartment, he paused in front of the mirror to make sure not a hair was out of place. He then practiced the smile that would later charm the girls at the club. For these nights of dancing, Bruce teamed up with fellow Wing Chun student Victor Kan. The two boys admired nightly singer Miss Fong Yat Wah from afar while they wooed women on the dance floor with their superb steps.

Soon, Bruce's charm caught the attention of Amy Chan, who became his first serious girlfriend. Bruce took Amy dancing whenever he had any money. But Amy quickly realized that dates with Bruce were a roller coaster of emotions. When they were alone, his quick wit would keep her laughing. But as soon as his friends showed up, Bruce turned into a show-off and somewhat of a chauvinist. His rude comments and macho behavior angered Amy and often led to heated arguments.

Bruce's hot-headed personality brought more than just lovers' quarrels, however. He found himself sparring in a fair share of street fights as well. Bruce usually carried a concealed blade or a steel toilet chain as a weapon, but he rarely used them. Most fights ended in ripped clothing and bloody noses caused by hands, fists, and feet. "One day one of us was beaten up by a gang from Kowloon," former Tiger Leung Pak Chun recalled in *Fighting Spirit*. "Bruce and the others went off to get revenge." At first, Bruce casually walked up to the gang, acting as though he wanted to talk things over. But as soon as he got close enough to the two biggest members, he hit them without warning. These two guys turned out to be relatives of a local Triad—one of many underground societies similar to the mafia. William Cheung's father, a high-ranking policeman, had to step in and prevent future confrontations. But this incident didn't stop Bruce. He continued to search out more and more fights—oftentimes for no reason at all. "And if he didn't win, he was furious," his sister Agnes remembered in *Fighting Spirit*. "Losing, even once in a while, was unbearable for him."

Schools of different fights styles often fought in "contests" with one another, and the wing chun school was no exception. On one occasion, Bruce challenged the choy li fut students to a fight. The two schools of fighters met on the roof of an apartment building on Union Road in Kowloon. The contest was set to last two rounds of two minutes each, with Wong Sheun Leung as referee. As the fighters took their positions, Bruce lined up with his opponent. The first round started, and Bruce's opponent, a boy named Chung, attacked him with a punch that Bruce palmed away. The next strike hit Bruce in the eye and knocked him off balance. Immediately in a rage, he counterattacked with a blitz of punches that stopped short. Frustrated, Bruce closed the distance between them and swung again, but his moves were too wild. Again, Chung struck him twice in the face. At the end of the first round, Bruce sat in his corner with a swollen eye and a bloody nose. He felt disheartened that he was unable to land any effective blows. Turning to Wong, Bruce said he wanted to quit, worried that he would be unable to hide the wounds from his father. But Wong persuaded him to keep going.

At the opening of the second round, Bruce narrowed his determination and set up in a confident, sturdy stance. He faked a few punches to throw his opponent off guard and delivered a straight hit to Chung's face. The strike pushed Chung off balance, and Bruce moved in with repeated punches until Chung toppled to the ground. Other fighters quickly intervened to stop Bruce's hits. Bruce broke away from them and thrust his arms into the air declaring victory. His proud moment was short lived, however. Chung's parents hurried straight to the police and reported what had happened. In order to keep Bruce from serious charges, his mother had to sign a paper promising her son would behave.

Unfortunately for Grace Lee, Bruce had little respect for the cops. He and the other Hong Kong kids felt they were treated unfairly. "The cops in Hong Kong never talked to you politely," he remembered in *Incomparable Fighter*. "They treated the kids, and even Chinese people, like dirt. Every time a cop opened his mouth, he'd swear at you. But if you were a white person, then he'd treat you completely opposite—he'd be polite—bowing and smiling." This treatment probably led to Bruce's dislike of the British as well. When he was growing up, the British were the ruling class, even though they were the minority. Bruce noticed how they all drove fancy cars up the hills to their beautiful mansions. Meanwhile, the rest of the population who lived below struggled to make ends meet. "You saw so much poverty among the Chinese people that eventually it was natural to hate the filthy-rich British," he said. "They made the most money and had the best jobs just because the color of their skin was white."

So for Bruce, changing his ways was out of the question. Finally, he was expelled from La Salle for his troublemaking. After looking at a number of schools, his parents finally settled on the exclusive St. Francis Xavier College in March 1958. Maybe there Bruce could grow into a respectable young man instead of a street-fighting punk. At first, it seemed as though Bruce might have found a new outlet for his fighting urges. One of his teachers—Brother Edward—encouraged Bruce to enter the 1958 Boxing Championships held between two Hong Kong schools. During weekend sessions with William Cheung, Bruce trained vigorously for the upcoming contest.

When the championships finally took place, Bruce was ready. With intense aggression and hard determination, Bruce blasted through the preliminaries, leaving three opponents knocked out in the first round. In the final match, he faced an English boy, Gary Elms, an old rival from King George V School. Gary had held the title for three consecutive years.

As the match began, Gary took charge of the ring, boxing in a classic style. Almost immediately, Bruce was up against the corner, swinging wildly. Even though boxing gloves are not the best tools for the subtler moves of wing chun, Bruce started using some of the blocks he had learned during his years of training. He then countered the blocks with continuous punches and a two-level hitting he'd been practicing. In the third round, he knocked out the reigning champion and took the title for himself. He was proud enough of this victory to make special note of it in the diary he kept of all his fights.

GANGSTER FUGITIVE

While Bruce may have been championing the boxing ring, academics were another story. Bruce managed to stay in school mostly by coercing other students to do his homework for him. Grace Lee worried about her son's future. It seemed Bruce was more likely to end up in jail than in college. Discouraged, Grace suggested to her son that he leave Hong Kong and claim his

American citizenship before his eighteenth birthday, when it would be too late. At first, Bruce resented the idea of emigrating, but his father thought it was the perfect solution to his son's problems. Eventually, Bruce too warmed up to the suggestion.

Bruce told Hawkins Cheung that he was going to the United States to become a dentist, but he would earn money by teaching kung fu. Cheung reminded Bruce that he had only learned wing chun to the second form and just 40 of the 108 practice

YIN AND YANG

All phenomena in the world can be expressed by the interplay of two forces called yin and yang. Yang represents the masculine or active creating force, such as heat, light, sound, and infinity. Yin is the feminine or receptive force, such as coldness, darkness, stillness, and the finite. Yin and yang are not concrete objects, but rather they represent the flow and interaction of energy that lies beneath every event that takes place. For example, a rock is yang compared to a rubber ball, which would be yin; the rubber ball becomes yang compared to a cheese ball; and a cheese ball would be yang to a drop of water. In martial arts, the stillness before a punch is yin. When the arm extends to strike, it becomes yang.

This concept is used to explain the way nature creates a third force—the living energy of all existence—known as the breath of life, or ch'i. In this process, the two forces come together to produce energy. For example, fire (yang) combined with water (yin) makes steam. The vapor is almost invisible, but if channeled it creates great force. In Chinese pictographic symbols, ch'i is steam lifting the heavy lid off an iron pot of hot rice. Another example is the way a bicycle works. Both pedals cannot be pushed at the same time. One must be pushed while the other is released. Therefore, the movement of pedaling requires both pressure (yang) and relaxation (yin). The two movements together result in a third force—forward motion.

movements on the wooden dummy. Still, Bruce considered himself the sixth-best fighter in the style. Nevertheless, he took Cheung's comments to heart and decided to learn a few more showy moves before he left.

Bruce went to see a man known as Uncle Siu, formally named Siu Hon Sang, who taught northern styles of kung fu. Sitting at a table in a local coffee shop, Bruce struck a deal with the teacher. If Uncle Siu would show him some new moves, Bruce would give him dancing lessons in return. At 7:00 the next morning, Siu began teaching Bruce two northern-style kung fu forms, a praying mantis and a form called jeet kune, or quick fist. But Uncle Siu found himself at the raw end of the deal. He expected Bruce to take three or four weeks to learn the moves, but it only took the young man three days. Poor Siu had barely got started on the basic cha-cha steps.

With the new kung fu forms under his belt, Bruce was ready to set sail for America. Prior to leaving Hong Kong, he had to apply for an emigration certificate at the police station. There, he discovered that both he and Hawkins Cheung were on a black-list of local troublemakers. He quickly phoned his friend. "We're on a known gangster list!" he exaggerated, according to *Fighting Spirit*. "I've got to clear my name, and while I'm there, I'll clear yours too." Apparently, whatever Bruce did to try to fix things caused more damage. A few days later, a policeman called the Cheung residence inquiring about "gang relations." In the end, Mr. Cheung had to pay to have his son's name wiped from the record so he could send Hawkins to college in Australia.

Just before Bruce was ready to leave home, he received a tempting offer. Run Run Shaw, the head of Shaw Brothers Studio—who employed his childhood friend Unicorn—asked Bruce to sign a contract with them. At first, Bruce wanted to accept the offer. But Grace Lee persuaded him to turn it down, insisting that his best future would be found through finishing his education in the United States. The day before he was to leave for America, Bruce went to say good-bye to his old friend.

Bruce confided in Unicorn how he felt like his father didn't love him and how his family had no respect for him. He finally decided that his mother was right—this may have been his only chance to make something of his life. He stayed in Hong Kong just long enough to win the Crown Colony Cha-Cha Championships of 1958.

On April 29, 1959, Bruce gathered all his belongings and prepared for his three-week Pacific journey. As he was packing, Grace Lee slipped $100 into his pocket. A few minutes later, Bruce walked into the room where his father was sitting. Hoi Cheun handed his son $15. Bruce picked up his bags and started out the door. Suddenly, Hoi Cheun called him back. When Bruce turned around, his father just waved him away again. Hoi Cheun was simply acting out a Chinese tradition. By calling Bruce back, he was asking his son to return for his funeral one day. Disappointed that his father had nothing else to say, Bruce walked out of the apartment, shut the barred door behind him, and stomped down the narrow stairway that led to Nathan Road. Later that day, the gangster fugitive boarded a ship en route to San Francisco. Although he was booked as a third-class passenger, he managed to spend most of the trip in first class by giving dancing lessons to other passengers. But back in his cabin, Bruce thumbed through his $115 and wondered if it would be enough to buy a dream.

4

The Return of Bruce Lee

On May 17, 1959, 18-year-old Bruce Lee fulfilled his mother's prophecy and his own namesake when he returned to San Francisco—the city of his birth. There, he stayed with a friend of his father's. Knowing his small allowance would quickly run out, Lee earned money the best way he knew how—by offering dancing lessons. One day during a dance break, Bruce gave a kung fu demonstration for his students. Standing in the crowd was Bob Lee, the younger brother of local kung fu instructor James Yimm Lee. Impressed, Bob hurried home and told the story of this dance instructor who knew amazing kung fu. James brushed off the ramblings of his little brother and didn't follow up on the tip. But only a few years later, these two martial artists would play important roles in each other's lives.

During his first few months in San Francisco, Lee met several local karate students who tried to persuade him to teach kung fu. But Lee insisted he first wanted to finish his education. At the time, he was determined to become a doctor and actually started buckling down on his math and English studies.

Hot tempered and obsessed with fighting, Lee quickly wore out his welcome. During the night, he would yell out in his sleep, even kicking and punching the covers off his bed. No doubt his Chinese host family grew uneasy. His mother, Grace, then called on the Chows, family friends in Seattle. They agreed to let Bruce come live with them while he went to school.

AT RUBY CHOW'S

Like Lee's father, Chow Ping had also been a member of the Hong Kong Cantonese Opera. While in New York, he was struck with an illness and could not travel with the rest of the company. Then, following the U.S. declaration of war in 1941, he was stranded in New York. A woman named Ruby nursed him back to health, and the two fell in love. They married and moved to Seattle, where they opened a restaurant.

Ruby Chow was a tough and independent woman. After meeting Ping, she flung aside traditional beliefs and divorced her first husband to marry her new love. When all her friends scoffed at her ideas, she ignored their advice and opened the first Chinese restaurant outside of Seattle's Chinatown. Her instincts proved strong, and she soon became an influential figure in the local community. Oftentimes, she served as a go-between for Chinese immigrants and police or immigration authorities. Neighborhood residents gathered at her restaurant, waiting for a chance to get Ruby's advice on their personal problems or money matters.

Before long, Ruby began opening her home to new arrivals from Hong Kong. She offered them room and board in exchange for light work and chores until they could find their feet in a new country. As far as Ruby was concerned, Bruce Lee was just another immigrant passing through. He would be treated no differently from the others. But on the other hand, Lee was in store for a rude awakening.

Lee assumed he would be a simple houseguest while he attended classes. And so, he was surprised to see his name as a waiter on the work schedule. When he arrived, Ruby led him to his third-floor room, which Bruce described as "no bigger than a closet," according to Bruce Thomas's *Bruce Lee: Fighting Spirit*. He immediately took a strong dislike to his kitchen duties. "Now I am working as a waiter for a part-time job after school," he wrote Hawkins Cheung. "I am telling you it's tough, boy! I always have a heck of a time!" The hot-headed street punk was not accustomed to taking orders from anyone, and customer complaints were not received with a polite smile. Time after time, he argued with coworkers and showed little respect for his boss and the hospitality of Ruby Chow. These two bullheaded individuals often faced off in open hostility. Ruby later commented in *Fighting Spirit*, "If I can't say anything good about anyone, I'd rather not talk about it. . . . I raised five children and I treated him like a second son. He was just not the sort of person you want your children to grow up like—he was wild and undisciplined, he had no respect. . . . [M]artial arts are supposed to be to defend people, but he used them to be aggressive!"

For Lee, however, growing up fighting was an important part of his culture, much like American kids learn to play baseball or soccer. In crowded Hong Kong, fighting and violence were common. Even today, many Chinese youngsters still practice kung fu. Although some people—like Ruby Chow—saw Lee's constant fighting as an aggressive obsession, he defended his way of life. According to M. Uyehara's *Bruce Lee: Incomparable Fighter*, whenever someone questioned the amount of time he devoted to martial arts, Lee would ask, "Are you a good driver?" If the answer was yes, he'd continue, "Do you carry insurance on your car?" Again, if the person said yes, he'd then reply, "Why do you need it if you're a good driver?" Most often, the response would be, "Because I don't know who is going to hit me." Lee logically pointed out, "Well, isn't this true of life? You never know who's gonna pick on you. You don't know when you'll get mugged. If it makes sense to carry insurance on your car, why not on your life? After all, you can always replace a car but not your life."

Bruce Lee felt a culture shock when he returned to live in the United States. Accustomed to street fighting, as shown in this still image from the film *The Chinese Connection*, he soon found that he would have to refine his ways.

In the beginning, Grace Lee sent her son regular allowances to supplement his small income. Occasionally, Lee would earn some extra cash doing odd jobs like stuffing leaflets in newspapers. During the day, he brushed up on the studies he'd neglected in Hong Kong. At night, he worked in the restaurant. Then, he enrolled in Edison Technical High School.

When Seattle held an Asian Culture Day at one of its annual fairs, teachers from Edison School asked Lee to give a kung fu demonstration. James DeMile happened to see a notice advertising the upcoming event. DeMile was a former heavyweight boxing champion for the U.S. Air Force who turned street fighter and led the Capitol Hill gang. Curious to see this young kung fu fighter, DeMile turned up for the show. Lee stood in front of the crowd wearing his round spectacles and a neatly pressed dark pajama suit. He told the audience they were about to see a Chinese secret that had always been kept silent from the rest of the world. As he demonstrated various kung fu styles, his moves looked nothing like fighting. The audience sat puzzled and restlessly awaited the "big show."

As Lee scanned the crowd, his eyes suddenly stopped on James DeMile. "You look like you can fight," Lee said. "How about coming up here?" Lee was right. DeMile looked like a fighter—all five-foot-seven inches and 140 pounds of him. As DeMile made his way to the front, he couldn't have been too worried by the slight young man. Lee explained that he was about to demonstrate a simple fighting system that had been created by a tiny Buddhist nun. Turning to DeMile, he asked him to throw a punch. DeMile thrust his right arm straight at Lee's head, expecting to send the shrimpy demonstrator flying into the audience. But Lee easily blocked the punch as he countered it with his own strike that stopped a hair away from DeMile's nose. The gang leader continued to attack Lee but without luck. Years of reflex, balance, and sticking hands practice had molded Lee into a worthy contender. DeMile appeared frustrated—he wasn't used to losing a fight. In street brawls, he often delivered a bloody and brutal defeat. And Lee—out to impress a crowd—wasn't exactly a gracious winner. At one point, he knocked his knuckles on DeMile's head and asked if anyone was home. Later on, however, DeMile swallowed his pride and asked Lee to teach him some moves.

There was another fighter in the audience that day—Jesse Glover, an African-American judo student. Glover was tickled to find out that he and Lee attended the same school. He later became one of Lee's first serious students. Before long, Lee attracted quite a following that wanted to learn kung fu. In the beginning, his classes met in Ruby Chow's parking lot after he was done with work. Sometimes, the group worked out in a backyard, and, in winter, a garage. His class was small, mostly made up of older men and judo trainees. The students were enthralled by this mysterious new form of martial art that was the ultimate in efficiency and deadliness. One student later recalled in *Fighting Spirit*, "I saw him give a gung fu demonstration during a street fair and was mesmerized by his blinding speed and obvious power, by his lithe fluidity and his perfectly executed moves . . . ." This man immediately sought Lee out, so he too could be taught. When he told Lee that he was interested in learning the art, Lee flatly replied, "Come by and watch sometime. If you're still interested, we'll see."

Jim DeMile and some of the other students used to drop by a local supermarket owned by Takauki Kimura, better known as "Taky," a Japanese-American who had been held in an internment camp during World War II. While he was in the camp, he took judo lessons from a fellow prisoner. The students bragged to Taky about this incredible young martial arts teacher they had come to know. "They told me I just had to go and see him," Taky remembered in *Fighting Spirit*. "Now, I'd seen martial artists in Japan who were older and more experienced so I didn't see how a young kid could be any better, but they insisted . . . As soon as I saw what he could do, I asked if I could join their club."

After Taky joined the class, training sessions were sometimes held in back of his supermarket. Oftentimes, the group joked around as they worked out. But if a girl happened to walk by, Lee was suddenly serious. At these times, DeMile usually tried to quietly slip away. When Lee wanted to impress a girl, he'd choose the most dangerous and menacing-looking student to "volunteer" for his demonstration. Naturally, DeMile was his first choice, and the street thug had a reputation to uphold.

Lee managed to attract the attention of Amy Sanbo, a Japanese American who like Taky, spent time in an internment camp during the war. At first, Lee charmed Amy with his amazing abilities and caring qualities. But she soon saw his darker, immature side. At parties, Lee would do one-finger push-ups to draw a crowd. When Amy accused him of being a show-off, Lee said he only wanted to see how everyone would react. Amy would turn away and scold Lee, telling him he quoted wisdom but didn't live up to his words. When the couple passed the poor or less fortunate on the street, Amy showed compassion for them. But Lee sneered at them, saying anyone who wanted to get out of a hole could do it. Lee's pompous personality finally dominated every aspect of their relationship. Their conversations centered around kung fu and his dreams for the future. When Amy expressed her aspirations of becoming a writer and dancer, Lee acted uninterested. He simply told her that she could find fulfillment through helping him achieve his ambitions. Still, when Lee proposed marriage to Amy, he was surprised she turned him down.

To earn some extra cash and perhaps pick up some new students, Lee started giving regular demonstrations in his neighborhood. His popularity landed him a series of television programs on Seattle's KCTS-Channel 9, the educational station. However, no matter how much Lee rehearsed his students for the shows, things sometimes went awry. During one show, Jesse Glover got stage fright and forgot what he was supposed to do. Face-to-face with Lee, he panicked and hit Lee in the face. An instant later, Glover found himself flat on the floor with Lee's steely glare above him.

Taky accompanied Lee on many of his demos. He watched his teacher put away some big guys but not with brute strength. One time, Lee told a story about an old lady whose house caught fire. Her most precious possession was a piano that stood upstairs. Without hesitation, the old woman rushed upstairs and carried the piano out. Later, it took four men to lift the piece. "Bruce could call up and harness that kind of energy at will," Taky explained in *Fighting Spirit*. "His power came from a tremendous base of internal energy which he knew how to bring out." Taky perceived this part of Lee's character as flexible, but there was a darker force hidden deep inside him that was desperately trying to break out.

THE BLACK SHADOW

As Lee was developing technique and form, he also was experiencing the inner changes that accompany a martial arts way of life. His restless sleeping patterns were signs of the turmoil boiling inside. Throughout his childhood and into adulthood, he walked in his sleep and even fought while he dreamed. All his internal struggles finally came to blows late one night.

In his room at the Chows', Lee tossed in his bed. Deep in sleep, he fought with a black shadow, which held him down for several minutes. Unlike his effortless fighting in class, this struggle had him drenched in sweat. But the shadow was not a demon or curse. Through his martial arts training, Lee had opened up access to powerful energies, energies beyond the ordinary. From an early age, Lee had learned that energy was neither good nor bad, but both—just as yin and yang are both light and dark.

That night, Lee was not fighting a ghost. Rather, he had come face-to-face with pieces of his personality that he had not yet acknowledged—anger, arrogance, and insecurity. He was actually wrestling with the darker side of himself. In the tarot, which is a system of cards used for fortune-telling, the "devil" card represents this archetypal experience and shows the powerful psychic energies that are set loose. In these readings, the devil does not represent an evil force but impulsive instinct and disordered energy. The devil teaches the person to accept all aspects of his nature—both light and dark. Another psychologist depicts this force as the "Shadow." The Shadow is the blocked energy that consists of repressed or negative feelings. When these forces are released, a great surge of energy follows that can be used for positive purposes.

Unsurprisingly, soon after this event, Lee embarked on a serious pursuit of self-improvement. He earned his high school

I CAN DO: LETTER TO A FRIEND, PEARL TSO (SEPTEMBER 1962)

Bruce Lee's dreams for the future were not just scattered wishes. He approached his dreams with amazing focus and conviction. In the following letter, Lee explained his way of life and future to a childhood friend in Hong Kong.

... There are two ways of making a good living. One is the result of hard working, and the other, the result of the imagination (requires work, too of course). It is a fact that labor and thrift produce a competence, but fortune, in the sense of wealth, is the reward of the man who can think of something that hasn't been thought of before. In every industry, in every profession, ideas are what America is looking for. Ideas have made America what she is, and one good idea will make a man what he wants to be....

I feel I have this great creative and spiritual force within me that is greater than faith, greater than ambition, greater than confidence, greater than determination, greater than vision. It is all of these combined. My brain becomes magnetized with this dominating force which I hold in my hand.

When you drop a pebble into a pool of water, the pebble starts a series of ripples that expand until they encompass the whole pool. This is exactly what will happen when I give my ideas a definite plan of action. Right now, I can project my thoughts into the future, I can see ahead of me. I dream (remember that practical dreamers never quit)....
I am not easily discouraged, readily visualize myself as overcoming obstacles, winning out over setback, achieving 'impossible' objectives....

Probably, people will say I'm too conscious of success. Well, I am not. You see, my will to do springs from the knowledge that I CAN DO. I'm only being natural, for there is no fear or doubt inside my mind.

Pearl, success comes to those who become success-conscious. If you don't aim at an object, how the heck on earth do you think you can get it?

diploma from Edison and scored high enough grades to be admitted to the University of Washington in Seattle. In March 1961, he started college classes. In the beginning, he enrolled in classes that were of particular interest to him—English, gymnastics, and wrestling. With a strong sense of where he was heading, he soon signed up for theater speech and speech improvement. Over his college years, he took courses in drawing, composition, social dancing, Chinese philosophy and language, psychology, personal health, leadership, and the Far East in the modern world. He supplemented his classroom reading with self-help books on positive thinking, making luck, and developing potential.

While at college, Lee still kept up his kung fu training sessions. By this time, he had attracted quite a following. However, he would not let his teaching come before his own learning. James DeMile related in *Fighting Spirit*, "It was more like he was saying, 'Here's what I have to offer—you take it. In the meantime, I'm going to be training and developing myself.'" Some of Lee's intensity spawned from basic survival instinct. In Hong Kong, Lee's contenders were his own size. In the United States, he faced opponents 70 pounds heavier and 6 inches taller, whom he referred to as "trucks rolling in," according to Bruce Thomas's book. To improve his techniques, he trained 40 or more hours a week. He traveled throughout California and the West Coast, even as far as Canada, to watch and talk to kung fu masters. When he could convince an artist to show him some moves, Lee found ways to make them more effective. He thought back to his training with Yip Man and began to wonder if much of what he had been taught was ineffective. The better he became, the less regard he had for traditional methods. "There's too much horsing around with unrealistic stances and classic forms and rituals," he said, according to Linda Lee's *The Bruce Lee Story*. "It's just too artificial and mechanical and doesn't really prepare a student for actual combat. A guy could be clobbered while getting into his classical mess. . . . It's fancy jazz. It looks good, but it doesn't work." He often felt that breaking bricks or boards with the edge of a hand was silly. "How often, I ask you, did you ever see a brick or a board pick a fight with anybody?" he pointed out. "This is gimmick stuff. A human being doesn't just stand there and wait to be hit." Although other kung fu teachers had little to say about his new techniques, Lee could back his words up with action.

Still, he clung to some traditions. He was proud of his Chinese dialect and insisted that his students pronounce the "kung" in kung fu as "gung." "The Mandarin or northern Chinese will speak with a 'k' sound but we use the 'g' sound," he explained, as told in *Incomparable Fighter*, "and that's how I spell it too."

Lee's exceptional abilities and somewhat radical approaches made a definite impression on many kung fu teachers, and his name spread. In 1962, California native Allen Joe planned a trip to Seattle for the World's Fair. Joe happened to be friends with James Lee, the Oakland kung fu teacher whose brother Bob took dance lessons from Lee when he first arrived in San Francisco. "Since you're going," James Lee said, according to *Fighting Spirit*, "why don't you check out this guy and see how good he is."

When he arrived in Seattle, Joe tracked Lee down at Ruby Chow's restaurant. He sat at a table until evening, waiting for Lee to show up. Finally, Lee walked in, as usual dressed sharp. Joe, seated at the table with a Scotch in hand, struck up a conversation with Lee about kung fu. Eventually, he convinced Lee to demonstrate some of his classic moves. The two men stepped out to the back lot. As told in *Fighting Spirit*, every strike Joe tried to land on Lee sent him "flying all over the place." Joe was impressed with Lee's smooth moves, which made other kung fu movements seem stiff and clumsy. After Lee finished his demonstration, he introduced Joe to his wooden training dummy, which he had named Bodhidharma, after the father of kung fu.

Back in Oakland, Joe bragged to James Lee about his session with Bruce. Several weeks later, James Lee wrote a letter to Bruce, inviting him to Oakland for a visit so he could see this wonderboy firsthand. After witnessing Lee with his own eyes according to *Fighting Spirit*, James had to admit, "This guy is good. He's unreal!"

BACK TO THE OLD NEIGHBORHOOD

In the spring of 1963, Lee began planning a trip back to Hong Kong. Shortly thereafter, he got a letter from the U.S. draft board, which had gotten wind of his travel plans and wasn't too keen on Lee leaving the country. Lee's American citizenship made him eligible for military service, and the draft board worried he'd skip out on his duties as an American. Acting on his toes, Lee immediately went to his English professor and asked her to write a character reference, assuring the draft board that he was an honorable man and would return. Finally with a green light from the board, Lee left for home in March.

During the summer of 1963, the Lee family, still in the apartment on Nathan Road, consisted of Mom and Dad, sister Agnes, brother Robert, a cousin, an aunt, a servant, and a chicken that pecked around on the veranda. Bruce Lee had invited his friend Doug Palmer to join him on the trip. Palmer, one of Lee's kung fu students, had studied Mandarin at college and jumped at the chance to travel to Hong Kong. Back in Kowloon, Lee showed his friend how exciting Hong Kong could be. They spent afternoons swimming off the sandy beaches or meandering through amusement parks. At night, they took in a movie or basked in the aroma of genuine Chinese cuisine while they listened to the bustling activity on the streets of Hong Kong.

Once again roaming the old neighborhood, it didn't take Lee long to fall back into his mischievous ways. And he was more than happy to show Palmer the ropes. One glance at a Hong Kong policeman was enough to fuel the lingering fires of anger and resentment to full blaze. He just couldn't resist playing a prank on him. As told in *Fighting Spirit*, Lee noticed that the policeman wore a red band around one arm. This sign meant he spoke some English, but Lee knew it was only rudimentary.

Bruce Lee poses for a 1973 handout photo. Upon his return to Kowloon, Lee fell back into his old ways.

At once, he instructed Palmer to walk up to the cop and ask directions to Canton Theater, knowing there was no such place. However, there was a Canton Road. "Canton Road?" the officer asked. "No!" Palmer insisted and explained that he was to meet a friend at Canton Theater. Palmer continued to ramble in English, thoroughly confusing the policeman. At this point, Lee walked up and asked what the problem was. When Palmer told Lee that he was looking for Canton Theater, Lee replied that he was going that way, too. The two young men walked off, leaving the cop with a puzzled look on his face.

Of course, Lee also had to show off a bit. He and Palmer created a skit to perform around town. They timed their routine so they would emerge from an elevator in the middle of a heated argument. Palmer took two roadhouse swings at Lee, which Lee blocked with his forearms. Then, Lee would throw a stiff uppercut to Palmer's stomach. Naturally, Palmer had to make sure he tightened up his stomach muscles to keep from actually getting hurt. Other times, Lee performed solo. He would act like a geek in front of a tough street punk, until the thug wanted to beat up this little twerp. When the punk finally took a swing, Lee would awkwardly block it and strike at the groin in a move that appeared to be an accident. In response, Lee would throw his hand over his mouth in pretend shock, shudder in his shoes for a moment, and walk off. Later, Palmer asked why he pretended to be an inexperienced shrimp instead of a real fighter. "A person can accept getting beaten by someone who is stronger or bigger than he is," Bruce explained, according to Bruce Thomas's book. "But if he thinks he's been beaten by a nerd, he'll be [angry] for the rest of his life."

Unable to take a break from fighting, Lee continued his kung fu training while in Hong Kong. Once again, he went to Yip Man, this time taking Doug Palmer with him. However, Lee cautioned his friend to simply watch and not let on that he knew any kung fu. Although Lee had kicked off tradition in the States, he did not want Yip Man knowing he would teach kung fu to just any race. In Yip Man's apartment at the top of a high-rise, Palmer watched amazed as the two slight men stuck hands for what seemed like hours at a time.

Finally, the summer drew to a close, and it was time for Lee to return to Seattle. On the way back, Lee and Palmer spent a few days in Hawaii. While there, Bruce was asked to give a demonstration at a kung fu school in Honolulu. At that time, like in Hong Kong, kung fu schools were strictly Chinese. But much to the students' surprise, Palmer climbed up on the stage with Bruce for the demonstration. It was clear from the demo that Palmer had some kung fu training. Afterward, one teacher coldly asked if Lee had been teaching Palmer kung fu. Now closer to the United States, Lee wasn't so concerned with keeping his wide range of students a secret. Still, he did not come right out and admit it. Instead, when the same man asked questions about Lee's technique, Bruce offered to show him. Through a series of blocks and counters, Lee literally tied up the man's arms. Lee further embarrassed the man by keeping his arms pinned while he explained each move to the audience. Clearly Lee was ready to resume teaching his students, whatever race they might be.

The Perfect Date

S late gray clouds hung low in the Seattle sky that September afternoon when Lee showed up at the University of Washington ready to start his junior year. He majored in philosophy, but his true passion was in the philosophy of kung fu. Early in the year, he asked university leaders for permission to use the men's gymnasium to give demonstrations. These showings attracted even more students for Lee. Before long, people began skipping classes in order to attend sessions in the gym or in the student union where Lee practiced kung fu moves while explaining the philosophy behind them. His clever wit and charming smile kept the crowds coming back for more.

One of Lee's regular students was a young woman named Sue Ann Kay. One Sunday afternoon, she invited her friend Linda Emery to tag along for the class. The two young women ventured to Chinatown, where Lee trained in a bare concrete basement. At first, Linda thought her visit would be a one-time shot. But like so many others, she was captivated by Lee's methods and also became a regular student. Sunday afternoons were the highlight of her week. At lunch, the group circled around Lee, listening to his deep philosophies and laughing at his jokes. Afterward, they'd head out for the theater to catch a samurai flick. On the way, Lee always walked several strides in front of the rest. From time to time, he'd suddenly toss an orange or some other object over his shoulder. The students soon learned to be on their guard, keeping their reflexes tuned to whatever Lee might spring on them. During the movie, he analyzed every scene and pointed out mistakes in the way the film was made. Later, he'd quiz the students on tiny details, such as which characters had been in the restaurant or the weather in certain scenes. In these ways, he taught his pupils to become more aware of what was going on around them.

Sometimes, Lee and his posse met outside the university on a grassy area surrounded by trees. On one of these afternoons, Lee managed to get a moment alone with the petite, strawberry-blond friend of Sue Ann Kay. He asked her out to dinner, without the other students.

Linda turned out to be the perfect date—she was a good listener! The couple ate dinner at the Space Needle's revolving restaurant, the twinkling lights of Seattle slowly spinning below. Throughout dinner, Lee rambled on about his plans for the future, how he wanted to open a real kung fu school, write a book about his philosophies, and become a famous kung fu actor. But so many things were holding him back. Still living at Ruby Chow's, he felt restless and trapped. His students had been pestering him to find a place of his own, where they could all meet and train. No doubt, he knew it was time to take this next step and venture out on his own.

JUN FAN GUNG FU INSTITUTE

While Lee was bouncing around the idea of finding his own place, his students offered to each pay $4 a week so he could support himself and pay rent. With a little luck, he found an apartment just off campus. It was the perfect spot—the entire

NEW WORLD HONG KONG

For Bruce Lee, a visit to San Francisco's Chinatown must have been like a trip home. Its brightly colored shops and scrolled Chinese signs resembled the ones on the streets of Hong Kong. The roadways were crowded with Chinese people, and the few whites who wandered about were probably curious tourists. Another image of the old neighborhood was the groups of young punks and the street gangs who lurked in the alleys at night.

During the 1960s, thousands of new Chinese immigrants came to San Francisco. Many of them couldn't speak any English. Unable to cope with school, teens dropped out. But without schooling and unable to speak the language, they had trouble finding jobs and became neighborhood misfits. Young hoodlums formed street gangs that harassed local merchants and tourists. At first, they stuck to purse snatching, but eventually they took up armed robbery and murder.

Some of these men were formerly Mao Tse-tung's Red Guards. Chinese Communist ruler Mao Tse-tung was perhaps the most powerful person who ever lived, controlling almost a billion people for more than 25 years. Backed by his army of Red Guards, Mao overthrew an army of more than four million and took control of Red China—a territory of eastern Asia covering more than nine million square kilometers. After Red China was finally under his rule, Mao had no use for the Red Guards. Some of them even became a nuisance because they were only trained to carry out orders to maim or kill. "These guys had no feelings at all," Lee explained. "They'd shoot a guy in the face as if they were shooting a dog."

When Mao no longer needed them, some of these thugs sneaked out to Hong Kong with the other refugees. Others managed to find a way to San Francisco's Chinatown. Knowing no other way of life, many immigrants created a New World Hong Kong, where, as in the old country, violence was simply survival.

ground floor of an apartment building that already had showers installed. He handed Ruby Chow his notice, and in October 1963, 22-year-old Lee opened Jun Fan Gung Fu Institute at 4750 University Way. He even printed up a brochure for his school, or *kwoon* in Chinese. In it, he advertised a martial arts method that was fast, efficient, and economical. But he also stressed that his techniques couldn't be mastered overnight or in three easy lessons. He did promise that kung fu would help them develop confidence, humility, coordination, and awareness.

Lee's personal living space was a windowless room in the back, sparsely furnished with some things he'd brought back from Hong Kong that summer. Here, Linda and Bruce spent most evenings, probably talking about kung fu and Bruce's future. Still, Linda kept their relationship a secret from her mother and father. No doubt, Linda's parents expected her to have Asian friends. After all, she attended a university where more than half the student body was Asian or African American. But she grew up in a strict, white, Protestant family. In those days, many people felt strongly against mixed-race relationships. Her parents surely would disapprove of the affair. Yet Linda didn't seem to let her parents cloud her feelings. Day after day, she found herself falling deeper in love with Bruce.

Even though at this time Lee's kwoon was small, he had high hopes for the future. "I may now own nothing but a little place down in a basement," he once wrote to a friend, "but once my imagination has got up a full head of steam, I can see painted on a canvas of my mind a picture of a fine, big five or six story Gung Fu Institute with branches all over the States." At last, in June 1964, it seemed as though his dream might come true. He and friend James Lee began discussing plans to open a second branch of Lee's Jun Fan Institute in Oakland, California.

By this time, Lee had quit his classes at the University of Washington. He had lost all interest in completing his philosophy doctorate. Instead, he seemed to get all his drive and fulfillment from kung fu. Lee sold his '57 Ford and shipped his furniture to Oakland. He then closed the doors of his kwoon and told his assistant Taky to reopen the school in Chinatown as a private club for a few of the regular students.

On July 19, Linda drove him to the airport. As they said a tearful good-bye, Linda probably wondered if she'd ever see him again. But Bruce assured her by saying that he just wanted some money saved up before he even thought about marriage or a family.

QUICK TRIP

The air was hot and muggy in the Long Beach Sports Arena, where the International Karate Tournament was held on August 2, 1964. The air-conditioning broke down, and, after sitting through hours of matches, the spectators shifted uncomfortably in their seats, blotting their foreheads with tissues. Event sponsor Ed Parker announced over the microphone that Bruce Lee would put on a demonstration of the little-known Chinese art of kung fu.

Lee walked out in a simple black kung fu suit and slippers. Just like at Garfield High School, he awed the crowd with a "one-inch" punch demonstration. Although some of his moves were quite impressive, Lee was against doing "tricks." His techniques had deeper meanings. The purpose of showing the one-inch punch was to prove that there were more powerful ways of striking someone than simply using arm and shoulder muscles.

Competing in the black belt division that day was Filipino martial artist Dan Inosanto. In addition to studying kenpo karate, Inosanto was also well trained in the Filipino arts of escrima and kali. After the match, he met Lee back at his hotel room to exchange ideas and techniques. When Lee demonstrated his moves, Inosanto grew frustrated. "I was completely flabbergasted!" he later recalled in Bruce Thomas's *Bruce Lee: Fighting Spirit*. "He controlled me like a baby—I couldn't do anything with him at all. . . . I'd lost to other people before but

Bruce Lee shows the intensity with which he performs his craft of Kung Fu. Lee was planning on earning a doctorate in philosophy but his love of martial arts hampered any further academic pursuits. Lee dropped out of school and began teaching kung fu full time, while pursuing an acting career.

not in the way that I lost to him: he was dominating the action completely, calling all the shots like it was a game!" That night, Inosanto tossed and turned in his bed. He wondered if everything he had learned was obsolete. He just had to learn more from this martial arts teacher.

For the next couple of weeks, Lee and Inosanto spent a lot of time together. Some days, they just walked and talked, while exploring old bookstores. Before long, Inosanto took Taky

Kimura's role as Lee's assistant and helped give demonstrations in the San Francisco area.

Lee and Inosanto organized a regular routine that included lightning-quick finger jabs, kicks, and punches that stopped suddenly, a hair away from the target. Sometimes, Lee would take on challengers, impress the crowd with thumb push-ups, and on occasion break a board. Eventually, Inosanto was taking punches and falls four days a week in demonstrations at Sing Lee Theater in Los Angeles. In the evenings, Lee taught some of his fighting methods at the Statler Hilton. Always on the receiving end of Lee's kicks and jabs, Inosanto marveled at this "devastatingly improved version of wing chun," according to *Fighting Spirit*.

Even with his busy schedule, Bruce wrote Linda regularly. His plans to build up savings before getting married were suddenly swept aside when he found out Linda was pregnant. Although surprised, he was far from disappointed. His perfect date would certainly make a wonderful wife. But marrying Linda quickly and smoothly would not be a simple task. Linda's mother still did not know about the relationship. All this while, Linda had been picking up her letters at a post office box so her mother wouldn't find out. Bruce agonized about how he would deal with this situation. Facing a karate black belt was one thing, facing his future mother-in-law might be enough to throw him off balance. He decided they should elope, retreat to Oakland, and then call Linda's mother with the news.

On August 12, 1964, Bruce made a quick trip to Seattle with a wedding ring that James Lee's wife lent to him. Unfortunately, after the couple applied for the marriage license at the courthouse, the news showed up in the local paper, as was the law. As soon as Linda's aunt saw the announcement, she called the Emerys to find out why she didn't receive an invitation. Word of the news exploded into arguments intended to pressure the couple into calling the wedding off. But Bruce stuck to his decision.

The family threw out dozens of reasons why they thought the two shouldn't marry. Linda's uncle complained it wouldn't be a "Christian" marriage. He also tried to dissuade Bruce by pointing out that Linda couldn't *do* anything. "She'll learn," Lee calmly replied, according to *Fighting Spirit*. More than likely, the Emerys were worried about marrying their daughter off to a man without a steady job or regular income.

Nevertheless, all arguing quelled when Linda's mother learned her daughter was pregnant. The family made quick wedding arrangements with the minister at the Seattle Congregational Church. The plans were so rushed that Bruce had to rent a suit for the ceremony and Linda didn't even get a wedding dress. No photographer was there for the big day, either. On August 17, Linda's mother and grandmother walked her down the narrow church aisle. Taky Kimura stood next to Bruce as best man, "the only person outside of the family to be invited," he later boasted, according to Bruce Thomas's book.

It was almost as if Bruce foresaw their humble beginnings. In a letter to Linda, dated October 20, 1963, five days before their first official date, Lee wrote to her:

> Linda,
> To live content with small means; to seek elegance rather than luxury, and refinement rather than fashion, to be worthy, not respectable, and wealthy, not rich; to study hard, think quietly, talk gently, act frankly; to bear all cheerfully, do all bravely, await occasions, hurry never.
>
> In other words, to let the spiritual, unbidden and unconscious, grow up through the common.
> Bruce

But deep down, Lee believed his dreams would one day bring incredible success.

To Infinity

Lee and his new bride moved in with James Yimm Lee and his family. Shortly after, James's wife died of cancer, leaving a young son and daughter without a mother. The five people in the house leaned on each other and soon became one big family. James and Lee went ahead with their plans to open a second branch of Jun Fan Gung Fu Institute in Oakland.

Although James was 20 years older than Bruce, the two men had much in common. Like Bruce, at the time, James was one of the few people in the United States with any real knowledge of the Chinese martial arts. He too had trained for years in traditional kung fu but was dissatisfied with its set moves, lack of style, and practical efficiency. Just like Bruce, he developed his own style. James fully understood the talent Bruce had to offer. No doubt, he learned more in the short time with Bruce than he had in all his previous training. James was a former state weightlifting champ, judo brown belt, and an amateur boxer. By day, he worked as a welder. He taught kung fu part-time on the side.

Naturally, these two martial arts deviators became partners and opened the doors to a new kwoon on Broadway. In the beginning, they barely had enough students to keep the institute afloat. But Taky insisted the new branch take all the profit from the old school in Seattle. This arrangement worked fine with Lee. Anyway, he never viewed his schools as money-making ventures. He wasn't out to simply attract as many paying customers as possible. He sought out students who showed talent, potential, and commitment. In his method of teaching, Lee favored one-on-one training. He didn't line up students in rows for group practice moves. He needed to grasp the strengths and weaknesses of each student and learn about his or her personality and natural abilities. Therefore, each pupil would progress at his or her own rate.

Lee saw kung fu as a way of life and took his teaching seriously. Mere technical moves are only the beginning of kung fu, he explained. A dedicated student must capture the spirit of it—harness it on an emotional and internal level. Lee refused to teach ready-made textbook moves. Instead, he encouraged his students to be alert and aware, feel what was happening at the moment, and solve the problems on their own.

For a while, Lee avoided scrapes with students of other martial arts schools, which had always been trouble in Hong Kong. In the institute's list of rules, rule number nine instructed students to use discretion when explaining the school's training methods to others, in order to prevent rivalry. But in early 1965, Lee got his first challenge from a Chinese kung fu instructor just across San Francisco Bay.

Wong Jak Man had recently arrived from Hong Kong to teach kung fu in the States. He had heard of a martial artist who would teach kung fu to anyone. Wong was a staunch traditionalist. He believed that Chinese "secrets" should not be taught to Westerners, who already had natural advantages of size and strength. Wanting to build a reputation for himself, he challenged Lee to a fight—and added a wager. The loser would have to close his school.

On the day of the contest, Wong brought along several colleagues and an ornate scroll announcing the challenge in Chinese. Wong must have thought Lee was no more than a big talker. When Lee was formally challenged, Wong expected him to back down. To Wong's surprise, Lee gave the document a shrug and was ready to begin. Seeing the young man's energy and excitement, Wong suggested, "Let's not make this a match—let's just spar together. Let's just try out our techniques," as retold in Linda's biography of Bruce, *The Bruce Lee Story*. "No, you challenged me. So let's fight!" Lee shouted. As a last-ditch effort, Wong and

Other Notable Individuals

CHAN VS. LEE

Movie star and TV actor Jackie Chan was born in 1954 to a poor family who had just moved to Hong Kong. When he was born, his parents could barely come up with enough money to pay the hospital bill and were almost forced to give him up for adoption. Like Bruce Lee, Jackie had much energy as a child, and his parents nicknamed him Pao-Pao, which means "cannonball." When Jackie was seven years old, his father took a job as chief chef at the American embassy in Australia. This promotion drastically improved the family's financial status. There, Jackie attended school at the Chinese Drama Academy, studying and working 19 hours a day under the famous Chinese Opera master Yu Jim-Yuen.

Like Bruce Lee, Jackie made his acting debut at a young age, starring in a lead role in an opera called *Seven Little Fortunes*. Although it was a success, the opera didn't hold much of a future for Jackie. About this time, the Chinese Opera started to decline, and he began working as a stuntman in Chinese films. At age 17, Jackie got his first chance to meet the famous Bruce Lee as a stuntman for *Fist of Fury* (released as *The Chinese Connection* in the United States) and later in *Enter the Dragon*.

After Lee's death, film director Lo Wei wanted to model Chan after the late kung fu fighter and changed his name to Shing Lung, which means his colleagues tried to throw in some last-minute rules. There would be no eye jabs, no kicks to the groin, and so on. "I'm not standing for any of that!" Lee said. "You've made the challenge . . . it's no holds barred. It's all out!" Unable to back down in front of his colleagues, Wong had no choice but to tough it out.

Unlike most of Lee's confrontations, this fight was not smooth, fast, or efficient. After a sloppy few punches, Wong turned to run. At this point, his colleagues stepped in to stop the fight, but James Lee cut them off. Bruce ran after Wong and punched him in the back of the head, but he couldn't seem to land a finishing punch.

"become a dragon." Today, Shing Lung remains Chan's Chinese name. In 1976, Chan starred in the movie *New Fist of Fury*, in which he imitated Lee. Unfortunately, Lee's style was impossible to imitate convincingly, and the film was a disaster. After several flops in Hollywood, Chan once again returned to Hong Kong films, where he rose to stardom. He was especially famous for his "three brothers films," which starred opera actors from his childhood. These films include *Project A, Project A II,* and *Dragons Forever.* Finally with some clout, Chan tried another run in America, but this time he would work on his own terms. In 1998, the film *Rush Hour* became Chan's first real U.S. hit. He followed it with an equally successful *Rush Hour 2* in 2001. He is also known for his popular cartoon series, *Jackie Chan Adventures.*

So who is better, Jackie Chan or Bruce Lee? Although Chan may be a better stuntman and comedian, Lee was a true martial arts master. Lee used his films to demonstrate fighting techniques and prove his theories. On the other hand, Chan often exaggerates his moves with stunts and wire work. No doubt, people are entertained when they watch Chan fight. But if they watch one of Bruce Lee's movies, they will probably learn something.

In anger and rage, Lee did something he'd never done before. He wrapped his arm around Wong's neck and knocked him to the floor. "I kept whacking him as he lay on the floor," Lee later recounted, as told in Bruce Thomas's *Fighting Spirit*. "I was so tired I could hardly punch him." Wong finally gave up, and his entourage dragged him off without a word.

Lee left to cool off on the back porch. He paced in frustration. He couldn't stop feeling annoyed with his fight. What should have taken just a few seconds took more than three minutes. More important, he felt weak and winded. How could this be? There was only one explanation: he was in less than perfect condition.

After this fight, Lee began analyzing his training methods. He revisited traditional styles and searched himself for answers. He realized that any martial art had shortcomings, but he couldn't accept this truth and move on. As always, he would have to find a way to overcome the obstacle, find a more efficient way, and concentrate harder on his physical condition.

Encouraged by James Lee, Bruce started an intense physical routine. Early in the morning, he would run several miles, often with his Great Dane Bobo, named after his childhood dog Bobby. He also used this time for meditation and mental training, which were at the top of his list. After lunch, he would take another run or ride an hour on his exercise bike. Many of his strengthening exercises focused on the abdomen. He even used a popular boxing method of training in which a heavy medicine ball is thrown at the flexed stomach. He also started exercising with weights, at first doing reverse curls to develop his forearms. Finally, he purchased a full weight set and used it every day. In addition to exercise, Lee added high-protein weight-gain drinks to his diet, plus ginseng, royal jelly, and vitamins.

Day after day, Lee pushed himself to the limit. Next to each workout exercise on his schedule, he would write the number of repetitions he set out to do. Beside some was the note INF, meaning "to infinity." For these exercises, he would push himself until he thought he could go no more, and then he would keep going.

Bruce also asked James to help him create some new work-out equipment. Today, a variety of practice equipment can be found in almost any martial arts school. There is usually a "heavy bag" for full-power punching and kicking; a "top-and-bottom" speed bag, which springs back if hit in a straight line; a loop and pulley device to stretch legs; and padded mitts to develop punching accuracy and power. Some schools have air-filled kicking shields to practice depth of penetration and kicking in motion. All these apparatuses were designed by Bruce and James in the garage.

Lee even revamped his wing chun wooden dummy, Bodhidharma. He spring-loaded the head and mounted it on a spring-loaded platform so it would fly back and forth and move unpredictably. Before long, he was so powerful that he could only go all-out on Bodhidharma. His strength was too dangerous for any person.

All the while, Lee was working on a new system all his own, one that would not falter like the last. Of course, wing chun was still the nucleus of his system. In a letter to Taky, he wrote, "My mind is made up to start a system of my own—I mean a system of totality, embracing all but yet guided with simplicity. . . . This is by far the most effective method I've ever encountered or will encounter. Anything beyond this has to be super-fantastic."

SCREEN TEST

On February 1, 1965, Linda gave birth to Brandon Bruce Lee at East Oakland Hospital. The proud father sent a birth announcement to Taky Kimura in Seattle. At the bottom of the card, he added, "A big healthy boy of course!" Becoming a new father was not the only excitement for Lee, however. He had recently gotten a call from TV producer William Dozier. Apparently, the owner of a fancy Beverly Hills salon, Jay Sebring, had been a spectator at the Long Beach Karate Tournament in 1964. One of Sebring's clients was Dozier. One day while getting a haircut, Dozier mentioned that he was looking for someone to play the role of Charlie Chan's son in a new series about the Chinese detective. Sebring immediately suggested an amazing young martial artist he'd seen perform in July—Bruce Lee.

Three days after the birth of his son, Lee sat cross-legged in the center of a set that resembled a suburban living room.

Linda Emery met Bruce Lee while she was student in his kung fu class. Bruce and Linda married and had two children, a son Brandon (shown in this 1966 photo), and a daughter Shannon. After Bruce's untimely death, Linda remarried and wrote a book about her husband's life, *Bruce Lee: The Man Only I Knew* which later became the inspiration for the 1993 feature film *Dragon: The Bruce Lee Story.*

He wore a black suit, a size too small, and a freshly pressed white shirt. A voice from behind the cameras asked Lee questions about his acting experience. Smiling nervously, Lee talked about his childhood movies in Hong Kong, his move to the States, and his newborn baby. Eventually, the conversation moved to kung fu. The interviewer asked Lee how kung fu differed from karate.

"Well, a karate punch is like being hit by an iron bar—whack!" Lee said, as retold in *Fighting Spirit*. He paused for a moment and gave a slight smile. "A kung fu punch is like being hit by an iron ball swung on an iron chain—WHANG!—and it hurts inside." The director then asked Lee to demonstrate some of his moves. An older member of the staff volunteered to be Lee's partner. As the two faced off, Lee joked, "Accidents do happen!" Lee explained that there were various kinds of fights—what moves would be used depended on the situation. "To the eyes," he said, "you will use the fingers." He threw a quick bil jee jab—thrusting fingers—toward the man's eyes. The old man barely had time to flinch. Lee then showed a series of punches that landed only an inch away from the man's face. His fists moved so fast that the air actually made a whooshing sound. Noticing the old man's uneasiness, the director asked Lee to back off a little. But Lee insisted the stage man was in no real danger. Next, he demonstrated kicks that flew as fast as the punches. The crew chuckled in awe. They just couldn't believe what they were seeing.

Lee went through two reels of film demonstrating his techniques and explaining the various animal forms, such as the praying mantis, crane, and tiger. All this he did while wearing his tight suit. At the end of his routine, he turned toward the director and made a slight bow. "Thank you very much," the director responded, according to *Fighting Spirit*.

A week after his screen test, Lee's father died in Hong Kong. Because of the new baby, Lee decided to make the trip back alone. According to Chinese tradition, a son not present at his father's death has to express great grief and sorrow upon returning home. At the mortuary, Lee crawled from the door to the coffin, crying loudly. His wailing would bring peace to Hoi Cheun's soul. While he was away, Lee wrote a letter to Linda. In it, he complained about not being able to shave or get a haircut, as Chinese custom forbids during mourning. "All in all I look like a pirate with long hair and whiskers," he said.

Two weeks later, Lee returned to Oakland. William Dozier finally called with good news and bad news. Unfortunately, the Charlie Chan series had been shelved. But because his new *Batman* series had brought such outstanding ratings, the studio rewarded Dozier with a chance to create a whole new TV series. *The Green Hornet* would use the same formula for adventure—a hero and his sidekick. Dozier offered Lee the role of Kato, the chauffeur and sidekick of a masked criminal fighter, the Green Hornet, known by day as Britt Reid. At signing, Lee received $1,800. According to Linda's biography of Bruce, he later joked, "The only reason I ever got that job was because I was the only Chinaman in all California who could pronounce Britt Reid."

THE GREEN HORNET

Knowing that he would receive $400 for each episode of *The Green Hornet*, Lee thought it was time he and Linda had a home of their own. In March 1966, the Lees moved into a small apartment at Wilshire and Gayley in Westwood, a ritzy area in west Los Angeles. Dozier planned 30 half-hour episodes of *The Green Hornet*. This show had once been one of America's most popular radio series back in the 1930s. Britt Reid—the Green Hornet—was the nephew of another fictional character, Dan Reid—better known as the Lone Ranger. By day, Britt Reid (played by Van Williams) was owner and publisher of the *Daily Sentinel*. At night, he traded his business suit for a green outfit and mask. Kato (played by Lee) wore a chauffeur's uniform and mask. This dynamic duo also drove their own version of the Batmobile called the Black Beauty.

Naturally, Lee was most concerned with how the action would be staged. At first, the fights were planned as slugging matches seen in most Western TV shows at the time. However, Lee refused to fight his way. According to *Bruce Lee: The Celebrated Life of the Golden Dragon*, he later recalled, "I wanted to make sure

"The Green Hornet" aired on ABC from 1966 to 1967. Van Williams starred as the Green Hornet, and Bruce Lee starred as Kato, his trusty sidekick. Although the series only aired for a single season, it allowed Bruce Lee to showcase his abilities to a national audience.

. . . there wouldn't be any 'ah-sos' and 'chop-chops' in the dialogue and that I would not be required to go bouncing around with a pigtail." He told Dozier, "Look if you sign me up with all that pigtail and hopping around jazz, forget it." Instead, he wanted to use the efficient style of kung fu. But Lee's moves were too fast for the camera to pick up, and they appeared only as a blur. "At first, it was ridiculous," Lee said, as retold by Linda in her biography of Bruce. "All you could see were people falling down in front of me. Even when I slowed down, all the camera showed was a blur." Lee suggested the fights be shown in slow motion—an idea that has been used many times since. He even agreed to do some flashy flying kicks for added excitement, even though Lee saw them as impractical. In a real fight, Lee pointed out to the director, moves like those would get you into serious trouble.

The series premiered on September 9, 1966, introducing the American audience to kung fu for the very first time. In the opening scene of act two, the Hornet and Kato come face-to-face with three hoods. Kato kicks a wooden box into their path, distracting them just long enough to get ready for attack. The fight is quick and effective, a few speedy kicks and powerful punches. In another scene, Kato beats some gun-packing criminals by shooting poison darts at them. The Hornet's big "sting" was a weapon that fired an ultrasonic beam strong enough to shatter metal. On the other hand, Kato mainly used his fists and feet. But in one episode, he introduced a Chinese weapon—the *nunchaku* (commonly known by the English plural nun chucks)—two short sticks connected with a chain.

Young viewers were amazed by what they saw. The real star of *The Green Hornet* turned out to be Kato. Lee began making personal appearances all across the country—on radio guest spots, on TV shows, at fairs and public parks, and at martial arts tournaments. Although he was a born show-off, Lee had limits on just how far he was willing to exploit his talents, even at $1,000 or more per appearance. He had no time for tricks like breaking boards. He even expressed his views on these stunts to the fans who wrote him letters. Surprisingly, nearly half of his fan mail was written by young girls. In one reply, Lee wrote, "Dear Vicki . . . Breaking boards and bricks are mere stunts and are not recommendable for anyone, especially a girl like you. Techniques are the main goal you should work at. If you want to break something, use a hammer."

As the series continued, Lee became a little frustrated with his sidekick role. Kato's dialogue was practically nonexistent. He wrote a letter to Dozier, graciously requesting more talk-time on screen. "I myself feel that at least an occasional dialogue would certainly make me 'feel' more at home with the fellow players," he explained. He even wrote a couple of scripts as suggestions. But time ran out on his ideas. Although the younger audience loved the show, adults preferred *Batman*. Older viewers felt Kato and the Green Hornet were simply unbelievable, which was ironic because the fighting skills on the show were probably the first "real" moves to hit television outside of the boxing ring. According to *Bruce Lee: The Celebrated Life of the Golden Dragon*, Lee got a note from Dozier that said, "Confucius say, *Green Hornet* to buzz no more." *The Green Hornet* series saw its final air on July 14, 1967, after 26 weekly episodes. The show finished with a two-part, crossover episode in which the Green Hornet and Kato teamed up with Batman and Robin.

After the cancellation of the show, Lee and Linda had to search for a new home, one they could better afford. They moved into a large, twenty-third-floor apartment nearby Barrington Plaza. Despite his popularity as Kato, no other roles popped up for Lee. He managed to earn a little extra cash, however, making guest appearances on *Ironside*, *Blondie*, and *Here Come the Brides*. Once again, he turned his energies to teaching kung fu. Although he never intended it, his techniques soon developed into a new martial arts style—jeet kune do.

Jeet Kune Do

One day, Lee and Dan Inosanto sat talking about swords-manship. In fencing, Lee said, the most efficient way of countering an opponent is the "stop hit," in which you parry and counter all in one move. In other words, when the opponent attacks, the defender intercepts it with a thrust of his own, much like Lee's kung fu techniques. "We should call our method 'the stop-hitting fist style,' or 'the intercepting fist style,'" Lee suggested, according to Bruce Thomas's *Bruce Lee: Fighting Spirit*. Inosanto asked how he would say that in Chinese. "That would be jeet kune do," said Lee.

Later, Lee regretted coining the name *jeet kune do*. He didn't believe he had a particular style of martial arts and certainly didn't like referring to his technique as a "style." Lee insisted, "There's no such thing as a style if you understand the roots of combat," as retold in *Fighting Spirit*. Lee's martial arts way was more like a religion. In fact, Lee centered his system on the same basic teachings of Taoism and Zen. His art focused on capturing the living spirit that flows through all real art, religion, and philosophy. But this spirit or enlightenment is only alive at the moment it is being experienced. According to Lee, the only way to understand martial arts is through actual experience. The spirit cannot be captured by someone who later reads, or writes, a description of the experience. Although Lee had been writing down his philosophies for quite some time, he never meant for his writings to be used as a "how-to" book for teaching someone martial arts.

Like Taoism and Zen, jeet kune do was a philosophy. It encompassed the idea of becoming one with nature and experiencing the harmony of yin and yang. The purpose was not to dominate an opponent but to achieve harmony with him. Lee believed in the intimate relationship between physical and spiritual energies, which he described as "body feel." In order to bind body and spirit, a person must first learn to relax. This concept was not new to Bruce; it was one Yip Man had stressed years earlier. Relaxation allows energy to enter the body. Only when all personal tensions are released can true relaxation be accomplished. Essentially, it is achieved through meditation, or *wu-hsin*, which can be done in both stillness and in movement. Wu-hsin means "no mindedness" but does not necessarily mean a blank mind. Instead, it is "a state of wholeness in which the mind functions freely and easily, without the sensation of a second mind or an ego standing over it with a club," according to *Fighting Spirit*. In other words, a person must let the mind think whatever it likes without any interference from the other thinker within one's self. By meditating daily, relaxation becomes a natural function. Ultimately, it can be called up voluntarily, even during a fight. When movement is relaxed, it becomes more refined and efficient.

In Lee's writings, he described three stages of learning kung fu. During the first stage—the Primitive Stage—a martial arts student knows almost nothing about the art of combat. In a fight, he would block and hit on instinct, or automatic reaction. At this stage, action in no more than an angry or fearful response. The second stage begins when a student starts training in kung fu. Lee called this phase the Stage of Art. In lessons, the pupil learns different ways of blocking and striking, the forms and kicks. During this period, he or she gains knowledge of combat but loses a sense of freedom. At times in a fight, the pupil will pause momentarily to analyze what is happening and to calculate a response. The action no longer flows by itself. The third and final stage is the Stage of Alertness. At this point, the student's training has reached maturity. He or she has evolved to react at an almost unconscious level, without any interference of the mind. As Lee explained in *The Tao of Gung Fu*, "Instead of 'I hit,' it becomes 'it hits!'" Lee further described this three-stage process as moving from ignorance to intellectual knowledge to cultivated ignorance. "In other words," he said, "before I learned martial art, a punch was just like a punch, a kick just like a kick. After I learned martial art, a punch was no longer a punch, a kick no longer a kick. Finally, after I understood martial art, a punch is just like a punch, a kick just like a kick."

Lee's stages of learning aren't exactly a unique concept. The same phases can be applied to anyone who learns how to play an instrument, use a computer, or drive a car. At first, a student can do very little but force a few notes out of a trumpet or type a letter painfully slow. After some practice, the actions improve but are still stiff and tense. With much experience, the subconscious takes over and movements become automatic. When a dog runs out onto the road, an experienced driver reacts instinctively. He or she does not have to stop and think how to use the brake.

Like Taoism and Zen, mastery of kung fu is approached through stripping away the "inessentials," not by acquiring more and more knowledge. Simplicity is the key. In her book, Linda said that Bruce compared this process to the work of a stone sculptor. Rather than building up the sculpture with clay, the artist chisels away what is not needed, revealing the hidden form inside.

KWOON THREE BRINGS BIG CUSTOMERS

In February 1967, Lee opened his third kwoon, in L.A.'s Chinatown at 628 College Street, just a few blocks from Dodger Stadium. Like those in Seattle and Oakland, this institute was an anonymous building with no signs out front. To ensure privacy, Lee even had the windows painted red. Lee and his assistant, Dan Inosanto, operated a strict membership, only teaching martial artists who showed talent. If Lee met a student who was serious and had potential, he was ready to teach for free. One L.A. student recalled in *Fighting Spirit*, "I was short of money and unable to pay for training. Bruce wrote me a letter saying, 'Come on in. Forget about paying until you can. You're sincere and that's what counts.'"

Lee encouraged his students to come in street clothes, saying they should practice in what they would actually be wearing in a fight. Although he liked to keep things relaxed in his school, he also demanded respect. "I know that a lot of us are friends," he told his class, according to *Fighting Spirit*. "Outside of school, I'm Bruce. But in here you call me *sifu*," which means "teaching father."

Long before, Lee realized that most forms of kung fu, karate, tae kwon do, and other martial arts were based on styles that were incomplete. One reason he refused to call jeet kune do a style was because he didn't want to limit it. Therefore, jeet kune do had no rules, forms, or set number of movement or techniques. In his words, jeet kune do was "the direct expression of one's feelings with the minimum of movements and energy. . . . My movements are simple, direct and non-classical," according to Linda's biography.

As she said in *The Bruce Lee Story*, on one occasion, a man asked Lee what he meant by "direct." Before the man had finished speaking, Lee tossed his wallet at the gentleman. Without hesitation, the man reached up and caught it. "That's directness," said Lee. The man acted instinctively and didn't waste time. Lee

Bruce Lee demonstrates three kung fu positions as Kato, his character from *The Green Hornet* TV series. During the filming of the show, Bruce Lee performed his stunts with such quick efficiency that the camera was not able to pick up on all his moves. The resulting images were blurry, and Lee would have to perform the stunts again at a slower pace.

continued, "And you didn't squat, grunt or go into a horse stance or embark on some such classical move before you had." He pointed out that the man would never have caught the wallet if he'd taken time to indulge in sophisticated moves. "If someone grabs you, punch him!" Lee said. Don't waste time on unnecessary stances. "You'll get clobbered if you do." In Lee's mind, classical kung fu was a thing of the past and would lead to any fighter's downfall. To make his point, he erected a tombstone in his Los Angeles kwoon that read "In memory of a once fluid man crammed and distorted by the classical mess."

Because jeet kune do did not have specific forms or movements, it could not be easily taught. Lee soon began to let go of his dream of opening a chain of kung fu schools across America. After *The Green Hornet* made him somewhat famous, several influential people tried to get him to change his mind. "I was even approached by several businessmen to open a franchise of 'Kato's Self-Defense Schools' throughout the U.S." Lee recalled, according to *Bruce Lee: The Celebrated life of the Golden Dragon*. "But I refused. I think I could have made a fortune if money was what I wanted. I felt then and still feel today that I'm not going to prostitute my art for the sale of money." He would only lend his name to a school if he could personally supervise the instruction or have it run by such trusted assistants as James Lee, Dan Inosanto, or Taky Kimura, whom he had personally trained.

But Lee found another way to make up for the money he would lose by not establishing a chain of institutes. The assistant producer of *The Green Hornet*, Charles Fitzsimon, suggested that Lee raise his rates at the kwoon. Instead of charging students $22 a month, he could teach students privately for $50 an hour. Lee was shocked by this proposal at first, but Fitzsimon pointed out that Hollywood was full of people who could afford to pay that price. Soon, Lee found out that Fitzsimon knew what he was talking about. Eventually, his rates rose to $250 an hour, and people like film director Roman Polanski even flew him to Switzerland for private lessons. Once word got out, Lee's school attracted some big customers. His celebrity pupils included Steve McQueen, Joe Lewis, Chuck Norris, and Mike Stone. The last three, between them, won every major karate championship in the United States.

Another one of Lee's celebrity students was screenwriter and producer Stirling Silliphant. Immediately, Silliphant could see that Lee was star material. However, spotting a star was one thing. Finding the right plots and getting someone to back him financially was quite another. In the majority of Hollywood movies, there are not many parts for a Chinese man, so something special would have to be created for Lee, and Silliphant was determined to find a way to sneak Lee into the movie business.

Silliphant managed to write a fight sequence into a love story called *A Walk in the Spring Rain*. The scene was set in the Tennessee mountains, and there just weren't many Asians in that part of the country. But he brought Lee down to Tennessee to choreograph the fight. The two brawny stuntmen in the picture were skeptical of little 135-pound Lee, who in all honesty did not look too tough. When the guys kept picking on Lee, Silliphant told him to give them a little sample of what a side kick can do. Lee handed one of the men an air shield and had him stand next to a swimming pool. "I'm going to give it a little kick," said Lee, according to *The Bruce Lee Story*. "But I suggest you brace yourself first, you know, I kick pretty hard." The stuntman rolled his eyes and shrugged off Lee's advice. With barely a whisper of movement, Lee kicked the guy right into the middle of the pool. The other stuntman, wanting to prove himself, quickly lined up to give it a try. He crouched down low and braced himself. A second later, Lee lifted him off his feet and landed him in the deep end. From that moment on, the guys no long picked on Lee—they loved him.

Lee also served as technical advisor for the detective thriller *The Wrecking Crew*, which starred Dean Martin and Roman Polanski's wife, Sharon Tate. Meanwhile, Silliphant was still trying to write an actual acting part for Lee. Finally in 1969, Lee made his first appearance in a full-length Hollywood film called *Marlowe*. Starring as Winslow Wong, Lee was in two of the best sequences. In one scene, Lee bursts into the office of hard-core private detective Phillip Marlowe (played by James Garner). He tears up the room, finishing with a high kick above his head to shatter a light fixture. In the other scene, Wong (Lee) and Marlowe (Garner) face off on the roof of the Occidental Building in Los Angeles. Wong leaps into a flying kick, and Marlowe steps aside just in time to send Wong sailing off the rooftop to his death.

Although far from the lead role, Lee had finally stepped into the film industry. He predicted he would one day make kung fu known throughout the world, and the best way to do it was by making movies.

CURSE OF THE SILENT FLUTE

To meet his ultimate goal, Lee had allies and ambition, and anyone who met him agreed he also had the necessary qualities to become an actor. Still, he could find no outlet for his dream. No one was willing to risk big money on a virtually unknown Chinese actor. Unable to wait for something to happen, Lee decided to take matters into his own hands and go to Hollywood with a movie of his own. Naturally, Lee realized a star role would be out of the question. But he figured if he had a stronger supporting role than he did in *Marlowe*, he could get the publicity he desired. Certainly someone would notice his talent and at last the door would swing open for him.

For several years, Lee had a recurring dream about a character on a quest, who in reality he understood was himself. These dreams struck him enough that he made some notes about them. He wanted to use these notes as an idea for a screenplay that Silliphant would write. The film was to be called *The Silent Flute*. In the screenplay, the flute was actually a metaphor for "a call of the soul," which only certain people can hear. In the story, the hero was a martial artist on a quest toward self-understanding. Along the way, he would encounter trials and revelations, fights with others, and battles with his own doubts and fears.

Lee would play several supporting roles—as animal characters or natural elements—that the hero would have to defeat. From time to time, Lee would also show up as the hero's guide, playing a flute. In the beginning, only the animals could hear his music, but by the end, the hero, Cord, would be able to hear it

Steve McQueen was one of Bruce Lee's many celebrity clients. McQueen was offered the leading role in the film *The Silent Flute* but declined the offer. Although their relationship fell apart, McQueen served as a pallbearer at Bruce Lee's funeral.

as well. Although the lead would be played by a big-name actor, Lee would still get to dominate much of the action.

At first, Lee wanted actor Steve McQueen to play the role of Cord, so he and Silliphant went to talk to him. McQueen shot down the idea immediately, saying he was too busy. But

Lee, enthusiastic about the project, continued to press him to take the part. "Be honest," McQueen said, according to *Fighting Spirit*. "This is a film to make Bruce Lee into a star. I like you, but I'm not here to make you a star. I'm not going to carry you on my back." Lee said nothing in response, and he and Silliphant walked out. McQueen's words burned Lee up inside. Once outside, he turned to Silliphant and said, "I'm going to be bigger than he is."

Next, they tried James Coburn, who agreed to take the lead role. Just when it looked as if things were a go, Lee hit another roadblock. Suddenly, Silliphant got cold feet and backed out, claiming he was too busy. Lee grew anxious. *The Silent Flute* had started as an idea to give him the exposure he wanted. Now, it was more of a necessity. If he didn't get a hefty paycheck soon, he was in danger of losing his new house in Bel Air. To make matters even more desperate, Linda gave birth to their second child, a daughter named Shannon, on April 19, 1969. Lee wasn't prepared to let the film die without a fight.

Finally, he convinced Silliphant to pick up the project again. But Lee's excitement was once again short lived. As usual one morning, Lee got going on his daily workout with his "Good Morning" exercise. He lifted a 125-pound barbell across his shoulders and bent over at the waist then straightened back up. After several repetitions, he felt a sudden twinge in his lower back. Over the next several days, he tried heat and massage treatments, but the pain only worsened. At last, he agreed to see a doctor. The diagnosis was grim—he had damaged his fourth sacral nerve, permanently. Worse yet, the doctor advised complete rest, adding that he should forget about kung fu—he'd never kick again.

A black cloud of depression descended on Lee. For three months, he lay flat on his back, the doctor's words echoing in his mind. His chronic back pain was aggravated by worries that Silliphant would shelve his movie, which at this point seemed cursed with bad luck. Still, Lee refused to accept the doctor's opinion. Through the power of positive thinking, he knew he could snap out of it. Six months after the accident, Lee finally pushed himself to train again. Even though he wasn't completely healed, he would act as if he was for the sake of the project.

About this time, Silliphant presented *The Silent Flute* to Warner Brothers, and the studio was willing to give it a shot. However, there was one hitch: the picture had to be filmed in India to use some tied-up funds. Previously, Warner Brothers had earned money there, but the Indian government wouldn't let it out of the country. Knowing it would be difficult to find a good location in India, Silliphant and Coburn shot each other a nervous glance. But Lee, who had done little traveling outside of Hong Kong and the West Coast, immediately made plans for the trip.

After arriving in India, the three men took a road trip across the countryside scouting for locations. They searched from New Delhi to the northern border but found nothing. Through long hours of heat, dust, and bumpy roads, their humor ran thin, and they started to get on each other's nerves. Silliphant and Coburn realized filming in India just wasn't going to work. But Lee wouldn't give up. They flew south to Madras and then to Goa—still nothing. Lee finally agreed to call it quits. He would have to face the fact that *The Silent Flute* would not be his big break.

Finally a Star

Despite the disastrous end of *The Silent Flute,* Stirling Sil-liphant still believed in Lee's future. He created a part for Lee in the pilot show of a new TV series titled *Longstreet.* He even named the episode "Way of the Intercepting Fist." With Lee's help, he wrote the story about a martial arts instructor who teaches a blind detective how to protect himself. Silliphant then handed the *Longstreet* pilot to Paramount TV head Tom Tan-nenbaum, who was trained in karate and who had seen Lee's demonstration at the 1966 Long Beach tournament.

In the script, Mike Longstreet (played by James Franciscus) witnesses a murder, but because he is blind he is unable to make a positive identification of the suspect. Still, he tracks the killer down and plans to unveil him. Before he gets a chance, a gang corners Longstreet on a dock and plans to drown him. At this point, Bruce Lee (playing an antique dealer appropriately named Lee) steps in to save the day, taking out the entire gang of thugs. Impressed, Longstreet wants to learn Lee's secret to fight-ing and begs Lee to teach him. Lee then instructs the detective on fighting methods, as well as his attitude toward life. But once again, Lee was forced to wait a while before filming of the show would begin.

Meanwhile, he flew to Hong Kong to arrange for his mother to come live in the United States. When he stepped off the plane, he was shocked at the welcome he received. Twentieth-Century Fox had recently released *The Green Hornet* series in Hong Kong and Southeast Asia—three years after it had aired in America. Dubbed in Mandarin, the show broke record ratings in Singapore and the Philippines. This time, Kato—not the Green Hornet—was the star. Immediately, TV cameras and newspaper reporters rushed Lee and bombarded him with questions. The silent sidekick was suddenly a star.

While he was there, Lee and his five-year-old son, Brandon, appeared on talk shows on both of the Hong Kong TV stations. Surprisingly, one host even talked Lee into doing a few tricks for the audience. Lee jumped and kicked at four one-inch boards. Splinters flew as he split them in midair. Even Brandon broke a board almost as big as he was. Charged up by all the attention, Lee sought out his old friend Unicorn who worked for Shaw Brothers film studios and asked him to probe his employers about a film deal.

In Hong Kong, the film industry worked like an assembly line. Studios would wrap up a picture in as few as three days. A big-budget film might take a week. The Shaw Brothers—Runjy, Runme, and Run Run—had pretty much set up the Hong Kong film industry. The Shaw Brothers Studios, made up of ready-made sets ranging from pagodas to concentration camps, sat on top of a windy hillside overlooking Clearwater Bay. Outside of Hollywood and Europe, Shaw Brothers was the biggest movie studio, producing two-thirds of the Chinese films in the world. The secret of their success was that films were shot without sound and later would be dubbed into whatever language was required. Not to mention, directors, actors, writers, and crews were all grossly underpaid. The studio owned 140 movie theaters throughout the

Mandarin circuit, which included Hong Kong, Singapore, Indonesia, Malaysia, Taiwan, and parts of Vietnam and Burma. In addition, they booked movies for 500 other theaters, including the Chinatowns of San Francisco, Los Angeles, and New York. Needless to say, if Lee could star in one of these movies, his goal to be known around the world would be off to a solid start.

Unicorn presented Run Run with a proposal from Lee to do one picture for the studio for a $10,000 fee. Also, Lee insisted on the right to make script changes and to be solely in charge of choreographing any fight action in the film. Run Run was not used to getting such strongly worded proposals. Ironically, although Hollywood thought Lee was too different, the Hong Kong studio saw him as just the same as any other martial arts

THE CHINESE ACTORS' SUPERHERO

Bruce Lee's plunge into Hong Kong filmmaking sent ripples rolling throughout the entire industry. Before Lee, Hong Kong actors always just took their wages and did what they were told. No matter how well the film did in the theaters, only the producers saw any of the profit. But Lee proved an actor could have more say in his career. He wrote, directed, and acted, started a revolution. Suddenly, other leading actors began demanding better pay and better working conditions. The effect trickled all the way down the system, to technicians and film crews. To Lee, it was not only fair for the key people to share in the profits, it would motivate them to always put out their best performance, which would benefit everyone.

When Lee's films gained international attention, it forced the whole industry to clean up its act. Hong Kong filmmakers would have to start making better films, with interesting plots and new effects. One Hong Kong newspaper commented, "Bruce Li is clearly an asset amid a local film industry bankrupt in everything but quantity." The era of four-hour-long, boring Chinese movies would have to face its merciful death.

actor. By the time Shaw Brothers responded to his proposal, Lee was already back in the United States. Run Run countered Lee with a seven-year contract for a measly $2,000 a film, the same as any other junior actor. Naturally, Lee declined.

Anyway, Lee had now begun working on the *Longstreet* episode. In the script, Lee got to relay his actual fighting method and philosophy. By far, this performance marked some of his most important work on screen. Just like teaching his real students, Lee teaches Longstreet how to listen to what is going on around him, how to feel his opponent. At one point, Longstreet has problems remembering all he has been taught. "If you try to remember, you will lose," Lee tells him. "Empty your mind. Be like water. Put water into a cup, it becomes the cup. Put water into a teapot, it becomes the teapot. Water can flow; it can flow or creep, or drip, or crash! Be water, my friend."

LANDING THE BIG BOSS

At the same time *Longstreet* aired in America, radio stations in Hong Kong were still calling Lee and then playing his conversations on the radio. One person listening to these talks was Raymond Chow of Golden Harvest Studios, a bitter rival of Run Run Shaw. He made Lee an offer—two pictures for a straight $15,000 fee, plus a one-way ticket to the filming location. It was enough for Lee to bite, and he quickly signed the deal.

Once Run Run heard about Lee's offer, he countered with a better one. But Lee had already signed on and planned to make good on his contract. Soon after, Lee flew to Bangkok, where he traveled north to the remote village of Pak Chong to film *The Big Boss*. Here, he met Raymond Chow for the first time. As Linda recounted in *The Bruce Lee Story*, when they shook hands, Lee declared, "You just wait. I'm going to be the biggest Chinese star in the world."

His first major film role was less than luxurious. Bangkok was in the middle of its hot season. Lee's small hotel had no air-conditioning to relieve the heat and humidity. With polluted

The Big Boss was Bruce Lee's debut martial arts feature film. The film cost less than $100,000 to make, and it brought in approximately $3 million at the box office in Hong Kong, alone. Bruce Lee was becoming a star, largely due to his work in this film.

water, no fresh food, and no mail service, it was hardly the star's life he'd imagined. Later in a letter to Linda, he wrote, "The mosquitoes are terrible and cockroaches are all over the place." Yet Lee couldn't complain too much. Finally, he had hit the silver screen.

The plot of *The Big Boss* centered around a Chinese community in Bangkok that lived in fear of Thai gangsters. The budget was less than $100,000, which at the time wouldn't even have paid for a 60-second commercial in the United States. Lee played Cheng Chao An, a young man who left a troubled life in China to make a new start in Thailand. Before he left, Cheng made a vow to his mother that he would not get into any more fights, and she gave him a locket to wear to remind him of this promise. Once in Thailand, Cheng is met by his cousin. On their way to his house, they stop at a roadside drink stand. There, a serving girl gets harassed by a bunch of boys. The cousin drives the troublemakers away with some fighting moves as Cheng watches from a distance, fingering his locket.

After settling in, Cheng takes a job at the local ice factory. Shortly afterward, two factory workers discover that some of the ice blocks are being used to transport drugs. The workers are suddenly killed. When the other workers become suspicious about their missing friends, they decide to go on strike. The big boss of the ice factory, a Japanese man named Mi, calls in his Thai goons to put down the uprising, and a fight breaks out. At first, Cheng is torn between helping his fellow workers and keeping the promise to his mother. But when he is struck by one of the thugs, he joins the brawl and in a series of stunning moves wipes out the gangsters. During the fight, his locket is broken in two. The film comes to a climax when Cheng takes on and defeats all of Mi's men and finally faces Mi alone. During the showdown, Cheng is cut by the villain's knife blade. He stops and tastes his own blood before the gory final scene. In the end, realizing he must pay for killing Mi's men, Cheng gives himself up to police.

While Lee was filming *The Big Boss, Longstreet* opened the fall TV season in the United States. Much to Silliphant's delight, it yielded good reviews. Tom Tannenbaum immediately tried to track down Lee in order to sign him on for more episodes. But Lee was isolated deep in Thailand, and no one could get a message to him. When Lee returned to Hong Kong, he found a pile of telegrams with offers to appear in three more *Longstreet* episodes for $1,000 a show. When Lee arrived back in Los Angeles, he was on the verge of something big. Paramount made a new offer, and Warner Brothers revived the idea of developing a whole TV series for him. Lee had lots of things to consider, coupled with his anticipation of *The Big Boss's* premiere. How would audiences react?

In October 1971 on opening night, Lee and Linda joined Raymond Chow and his partner Leanord Ho for the midnight premiere of the film. When the film ended, the audience sat breathless for a few seconds in stunned silence. The silence was followed by an uproar of chaos. An excited crowd practically mobbed Lee as he tried to leave the theater. Within three weeks of its release, *The Big Boss* smashed local box-office records, taking in more than $3 million in Hong Kong. The film played 875 times in Hong Kong before being released in the whole Mandarin circuit. Even in America, the film was a hit. According to *The Bruce Lee Story*, one critic wrote, "That film is the finest action job of Bruce Lee's career. . . . I would match it against the best of Clint Eastwood, Steve McQueen, or the various James Bonds." Naturally, Run Run Shaw was kicking himself for his oversight. As retold in *Fighting Spirit*, "Bruce Lee was just another actor," Run Run sighed. "How could I know?"

FISTS OF FURY

In 1971 before the premiere of *The Big Boss*, Lee was already working on his second film, *Fists of Fury*. (Later, the film was released in the United States as *The Chinese Connection*.) The story begins in 1908, with a real historical event—the death of martial arts teacher Ho Yuan Chia. Around 1900, the Japanese established a strong political presence in Shanghai. With extraordinary strength, Ho once defeated an entire troop of Japanese

A movie poster for *Fists of Fury* showcases Bruce Lee's kung fu talents. At its time of release, *Fists of Fury* was the highest-grossing film in Hong Kong, only to be outdone by Bruce Lee's second film *The Chinese Connection*.

challengers. In the story, Lee plays Chen Chen, a former student of the master. At the funeral, Chen throws himself into the open grave and claws at the coffin. "How can a healthy man die?" he wails.

Later, a friend of the Japanese martial arts association insults the old master's memory with a tablet-like banner that reads "to the sick Nation of Eastern Asia." Enraged, Chen goes to the Japanese club and single-handedly defeats the entire group and smashes the banner. Now an outlaw, Chen goes into hiding. Chen also learns that two spies actually poisoned his teacher. He kills the men and hangs their bodies from a lamppost. Determined to avenge his teacher's death, Chen goes on a killing rampage, desperate to get all the men responsible for the murder. At the end, Chen faces an armed police line where he meets a glorious death, running into a volley of the persecutors' bullets.

After six weeks of production, the film was ready to hit theaters. The opening scenes plunged deep into the heart of popular Chinese feelings. When Chen confronted his Japanese opponents and said, "Now you listen to me, and I'll only say this once: we are not sick men," audiences went wild. In its first four weeks, *Fists of Fury* broke records previously set by *The Big Boss*, earning more than $4 million in Hong Kong. On the streets, sold-out tickets went for $50 a pop. Lee had risen to stardom almost overnight. Suddenly, he was unable to walk down the street or sit down at a restaurant without drawing a crowd. This time, he attracted fans of all ages, not just youngsters. According to *Fighting Spirit*, one middle-aged moviegoer commented, "He's in a league of his own. It's a question of body movement and choreography, the timing, the overcoming of human limitations." On the other hand, he was constantly pestered by cocky street punks who now wanted to challenge him to a fight. Either way, Lee's kung fu was finally getting the worldwide attention he had hoped for.

9

Way of the Dragon

After *The Big Boss* and *Fist of Fury,* Lee found himself answering to accusations that his films glorified violence. In one *Big Boss* scene, Lee splits a man's head open with a saw (the scene was censored in the United Kingdom). "I do not believe in playing up violence in films," Lee said, as told in *Bruce Lee: The Celebrated Life of the Golden Dragon.* Lee claimed the fighting in his films was "action," not violence. "An action film borders between reality and fantasy," he explained. "If I were to be completely realistic in my films, you would call me a violent, bloody man. I would simply destroy my opponent by tearing his guts out." But this admission of fantasy left Lee uneasy. He really wanted to make films that were serious, philosophical, *and* entertaining. As it was, Lee's audiences wanted action that portrayed him as a type of superhero. Still, Lee knew that if he expressed what he really wanted in his films, chances were most audiences wouldn't understand.

At this time, Lee also anxiously awaited word from Warners and the ABC network about a TV series called *The Warrior.* The

The image above is taken from the film *Game of Death*. Robert Clause, who directed *Enter the Dragon*, signed on to direct an entirely new film using old scenes from *Game of Death* intermixed with new footage. The end product was released in 1978, five years after Lee's death.

show featured the adventures of a Shaolin warrior-priest, a fugitive from a murder in Imperial China, who used his kung fu skills against outlaws of the Old West. Lee desperately wanted the lead part of Kwai Chang Caine.

On December 7, 1971, according to Bruce Thomas's *Fighting Spirit*, Lee received a telegram from Warners stating that "due to pressures from the network regarding casting" he had been dropped from *The Warrior* series, which had been renamed *Kung Fu*. Amazingly, here was a Chinese story with a Chinese man as the main character, and Lee was axed because he looked *too* Chinese. Some other reasons the studio gave were that he was too short, had too strong of a Chinese accent, and was not a big enough name to carry a weekly TV series in the States. Ironically, *Kung Fu*—a show named after the martial art form that Lee single-handedly introduced to the American public— would star some other actor.

Eventually on February 22, 1973, ABC's movie of the week was the pilot episode for the *Kung Fu* series. The lead role had been given to David Carradine, who looked just a little Chinese. The only knowledge of kung fu Carradine had was that he had heard the expression mentioned—twice. In fact, most of the early action featured judo moves because the technical advisor also knew very little about kung fu. It must have pained Lee to see this art form so grossly misrepresented, how much he could actually stand to watch. By this time, however, Lee had already starred in three box-office hits and was working on his first American film.

It didn't take Lee too long to bounce back from his rejection letter that December. He immediately threw himself into another project, a film he wrote himself called *Way of the Dragon*.

A SMASH HIT

So far, Lee had gotten little help relying on others to meet his goals. He decided it was time to take matters into his own hands. He planned to make *Way of the Dragon* almost entirely by himself. To get some background, he read dozens of books about all aspects of the filmmaking industry. He intended to write, produce, direct, cast, choreograph, scout locations, choose wardrobe, and star in the film. He even played percussion for the soundtrack music. For the base storyline, Lee drew on his own past—leaving Hong Kong for a new country, becoming a waiter at Ruby Chow's, and even using his childhood nickname Dragon in the title.

At first, Lee offered Joe Lewis the opposing role in the film. Upon hearing the idea, Lewis immediately thought Lee was out to prove that Asian martial art was superior to Western. As told in *Fighting Spirit*, he claimed all Lee wanted was to cast him as "a big, strong, muscular, blue-eyed, blond-haired, all-American punch bag" and quickly declined. But Lee insisted it was a compliment to Lewis's talent. It wasn't easy finding a Western martial artist who was fast enough to convincingly fight him. Still, Lewis must have thought the idea of an Asian defeating a Caucasian was ludicrous. "Bruce knew he was asking me to get involved with a movie in which I got my butt beat by a little 128-pound Chinese guy who had never been in the ring."

But Lee wasn't completely out of choices. Next, he asked Chuck Norris to take the role. Norris was one of the few martial artists quick enough to stand up to Lee. And to Lee's delight, he jumped at the chance.

In the movie, Lee plays a country hick named Tang Lung (China Dragon) who leaves Hong Kong and travels to Rome. There, he learns that his cousin has inherited a restaurant on a piece of land wanted by the mob. In order to defend themselves against the gangsters, all the waiters had been learning karate. Lung walks into one of these training sessions just as one waiter (played by Unicorn) is drilling the others (Lee's adopted brother Wu Ngan is in the bunch). An argument arises about the differences in fighting systems. "It doesn't matter where it comes from," Lung interrupts, "you can learn to use it."

The picture was filmed as a comedy and features a number of humorous scenes. In one, Lung stops at a restaurant, and unable to speak the language ends up ordering four bowls of soup.

Return of the Dragon, also known as *Way of the Dragon*, was Bruce Lee's third feature film and starred a young Chuck Norris. Bruce Lee took complete control of the movie by writing, directing, producing, and starring in the film.

The film was cut with long pauses to allow for laughter, and the soundtrack was complete with "wah-wah" sounds and booms from the timpani.

Still, *Way of the Dragon* features some outstanding fight scenes and even a few kung fu lessons. Later on in the film, thugs show up at the restaurant to bully customers. Lung ends up battling them outside, where he shows off some of Lee's signature moves. After seeing Lung's amazing feats, the waiters vow to give up karate and take up Chinese fighting. In another scene, Lung battles the gangsters with nunchaku (once again, the United Kingdom censored this scene, so much so that the action makes little sense). The nunchaku is a weapon more dangerous for an inexperienced user than it is to his opponent. Lee used this well-known fact for comic purposes. After watching

Lung expertly whirl the nunchaku around in the air, an Italian hood grabs a pair. As he swings at Lung, he knocks himself out.

Now that Lung has wiped out all the local hoods, the mob boss pulls in ringers, played by Korean hapkido master Wong In Sik and karate stars Bob Wall and Chuck Norris. In the Western version of the film (later released), Norris's character is named Colt. By offering a truce, the hired fighters lure Lung into a trap and a battle ensues. Lung takes care of the first two opponents and is left to face Colt. In the final scene, the backdrop setting suddenly shifts from a rolling countryside to the arches of the Coliseum, a scene Lee managed to film illegally. As Lung prepares to fight his ultimate enemy, the only witness is a tiny kitten. Again, the scene has its funny moments, like when Lung rips a fistful of hair off Colt's chest. Yet most critics agree this fight scene was the best Lee ever put on film.

Lee was careful to make sure the climactic scene was not a one-sided fight. At first, Colt has the upper hand. About halfway through, Lung delivers a series of devastating hits and begins to turn things around. The attack ends with a final flurry of blows, finishing with Lung breaking Colt's neck. Lung then gently lowers Colt's body to the ground and places his enemy's jacket and black belt over the corpse, honoring the warrior's code to treat a worthy opponent with respect. The final image is striking—Lung defeats a Caucasian fighter in the Western world's greatest arena.

With a $130,000 budget, the first team arrived in Rome on May 4, 1972. It was the first Hong Kong–based picture to be filmed in Europe. Full shooting began on May 10 with Lee buzzing the crew to different locations around Rome. As a director, Lee demanded the same level of commitment from everyone else that he had for himself. He pushed them to work 14-hour days, seven days a week. On one day alone, they shot an unbelievable 62 setups in Rome's airport. Of course, the fighting scenes were different. Lee spent 45 hours filming his fight scene with Norris. Not surprising, his choreographed directions for this scene took up nearly one-fourth of the script. When it came to fighting, Lee was particular. Any unconvincing action had to be reshot.

After finishing, Lee bragged to his friends that *Way of the Dragon* would be a smash hit on the Mandarin circuit. He boldly predicted it would break all previous box-office records, bringing in a cool $5 million in Hong Kong alone. He was wrong—it grossed $5.5 million in the first three weeks. However, he had no plans of releasing it in the United States. He wrote the script with the Chinese culture in mind. Although his humor had Eastern audiences rolling in the aisles, Lee feared Westerners might find it a bit corny.

His smash hit catapulted him to a whole new level of stardom. He was constantly signing autographs and fighting off a mess of paparazzi. The great success he strove for came at a high

ASIAN IDOL OR AMERICAN STAR?

As his career progressed, Bruce Lee must have felt pulled in two directions. Lee grew up in Hong Kong and became famous in Hong Kong before the United States finally embraced his talents. Yet he had many ties to his country of birth—his dear friends Taky, James Lee, and Dan. Not to mention, he developed his philosophies and techniques while living in the States. Lee had a deep respect for the American film industry, and he wanted to bring the true art of kung fu to the big screen. In an interview with Canadian news reporter Pierre Berton, Lee seems to blend his Chinese ancestry with his American life into one identity. Both parts of his history and experience are woven together, so he is neither one nor the other.

Berton: Are you going to stay in Hong Kong and be famous, or are you going to the United States and be famous?

Lee: I'm gonna do both. Because I have already made up my mind that in the United States, I think something of the Oriental, I mean the true Oriental, should be shown.

Berton: Hollywood sure as heck hasn't.

price. "The biggest disadvantage is losing your privacy," Lee said according to *The Bruce Lee Story*. "It's ironic but we all strive to become successful, but once you're there, it's not all rosy. There's hardly a place in Hong Kong where I can go without being stared at or people asking me for autographs." His mother's prediction of an actor's life turned out to be painfully accurate. Out in public, Lee often disguised himself in dark glasses and a beard. Lee also bought a house in Hong Kong so he'd have a place to retreat. The Lees found a two-story house at 41 Cumberland Road in the Kowloon Tong area. The 11-room house would have been considered average in Beverly Hills, but in Hong Kong it was a palace. An eight-foot wall and wrought-iron gates kept out the paparazzi. And inside, he could at least enjoy a bit of peace while

Lee: You better believe it, man. I mean it's always the pigtail and the bouncing around, chop-chop, you know, with the eyes slanted and all that.

Berton: Let me ask you about the problems that you face as a Chinese hero in an American series. Have people come up to you in the industry and said, "Well, we don't know how the audience is going to take a non-American?"

Lee: Well, the question has been raised. In fact it is being discussed, and that is why *The Warrior* is probably not going to be on. . . . They think, business-wise, it's a risk. And I don't blame them. . . . If I were the man with the money, I would probably have my own worry whether or not the acceptance would be there.

Berton: How about the other side of the coin: is it possible that you are—well, you're fairly hip and fairly Americanized—are you too Western for Oriental audiences?

Lee: I have been criticized for that.

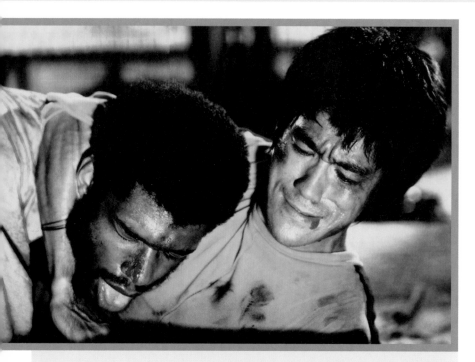

Bruce Lee holds basketball legend Kareem Abdul-Jabbar in a headlock for the movie *Game of Death*, the film that Lee was shooting at the time of his death. Before he died, 54 minutes of footage was already shot. The documentary *Bruce Lee: A Warrior's Journey* features some of the remaining footage from *Game of Death*.

strolling through his Japanese garden, listening to the bubbling sounds of the stream that twisted through the yard and emptied into a goldfish pond.

Lee kept to himself as much as possible. He avoided social gatherings, which he never liked much, even before he became famous. "I'm not that kind of cat," Lee admitted, as retold by Linda in *The Bruce Lee Story*. "I don't drink or smoke and those events are many times senseless. I don't like to wear stuffy clothes and be at places where everyone is trying to impress everybody else." With *Way of the Dragon* done, Lee had planned to take some time off to rest. But in October 1972, he heard that basketball star Kareem Abdul-Jabbar was in Hong Kong. Immediately, he arranged some action sequences that could be used in his next film, *Game of Death*. Lee must have wondered how he would go about fighting a man more than seven feet tall.

Lee had met Jabbar in 1967. Back then, he was known as Big Lew Alcindor (Kareem Abdul-Jabbar was the name he took when he converted to Islam). Like so many others, Jabbar became one of Lee's celebrity students. At the time Jabbar was in Hong Kong, Lee had not yet written a script for *Game of Death*. But the story had been brewing in Lee's imagination ever since he laid eyes on the temples of Nepal in northern India. In the story, a national treasure is stolen and hidden on the top floor of a pagoda, which is actually a school for different martial arts traditions. Each floor is defended by the master of a particular tradition, and Lee—the hero in the story—must defeat each opponent. In the final scene titled "The Temple of the Unknown," Lee—master of anything that works—fights Jabbar—master of no style. For this battle, all rules are thrown out, and each master must rely entirely on his wits and natural fighting skills. During Jabbar's stay in Hong Kong, the two men spent a week sparring in front of the cameras. Determined to make the fight utterly convincing, Lee practiced one particular kick 300 times. Despite the fact that Jabbar was a giant next to Lee—two feet taller—they managed to capture some intriguing and oddly elegant footage.

Just as he was getting started, Lee had to cut short his *Game of Death* filming. Back in Hollywood, Warner Brothers finally decided it was safe to sign Bruce Lee to a project. They offered him a starring role in a U.S.-made film in which he could have complete control over all the fight scenes. He immediately flew back to the States to finalize the deal. As soon as the ink was dry on the contract, Lee made a quick phone call to Steve McQueen from his room at the Beverly Wilshire hotel. He just had to tell McQueen the news—he was now just as famous as the matinee idol. In February 1973, Lee again left for Hong Kong, where he would begin filming his first American feature film—*Enter the Dragon*.

10

Exit the Dragon

The $500,000 budgeted for *Enter the Dragon* would barely have paid for one episode of a Hollywood TV show, but by Hong Kong's standards it was enough to film a trilogy. The American cast and crew arrived in Hong Kong in early February 1973. On the first night, Lee insisted on taking the film's director, Robert Clouse, to one of his movies. Lee told Clouse it was to show him Chinese culture. But the real reason was much more personal. When they first met, Clouse knew nothing of Lee's reputation. Lee wanted to prove to the director just what kind of actor he was working with.

In *Enter the Dragon*, Bruce fittingly plays "Lee," an author and the top martial arts student of a Shaolin temple in the countryside near Hong Kong. The plot mirrors the James Bond film *Dr. No* in that Lee is met by an intelligence agent named Braithwaite. (Reportedly, Clouse took an instant dislike to Lee and chose the name Braithwaite to frustrate the actor, because he knew Lee would have trouble pronouncing it.) The agent asks Lee to enter a martial arts tournament that is going to be held on a creepy private island off the coast of Hong Kong. Lee's mission is to flush out a former Shaolin student, Han, who pretends to run a martial arts school on the island, which is really a base for his drug and prostitution operation. According to Braithwaite, Han is so afraid of being assassinated he has a metal scanner covering the entire island to prevent any guns from getting inside.

One night on the island, Lee goes for a stroll. He discovers the massive underground opium-processing operation where Han also drugs young women, keeping them prisoners until they can be used for prostitution. The tournament starts the following morning. Lee fights a powerful contender named Oharra. Realizing he is going to lose, Oharra tries attacking Lee with two broken bottles, but Lee kills him with a powerful kick. That night, Lee again ventures into the caverns. He fights his way into the radio room, only to be captured by Han, but not before he manages to call Braithwaite.

The next morning, the tournament resumes. Han sets Lee up against a tough fighter, certain Lee will go to his death. As it turns out, the contender is Lee's ally. When Han finds out, he sends his thugs to the tournament to kill them both. Meanwhile, an undercover agent on the island, Mei Ling, sneaks into the cavern and frees the prisoners. Seeking revenge, the prisoners storm the tournament hall and battle Han's men. In all the chaos, Han manages to escape. Lee pursues him and corners the criminal in a maze of mirrors. They engage in a grueling fight that ends with Han being impaled on one of his own spears. Just then, helicopters circle the sky above the island, carrying soldiers sent by Braithwaite to finish the job.

From the first day of filming, nothing seemed to go right. Using both American and Chinese crews opened up a whole array of miscommunications. When they wanted to film a feast scene, there was no food around. Another time, someone was supposed to order doves. Instead, frogs arrived on the set. Extras showed up one day but ended up sitting around for hours, then wouldn't show up the next day. Not only was there a shortage of translators, but oftentimes there were no Chinese words for English jargon and technical terms, and vice versa. American crews quickly found out that Hong Kong was not Hollywood. There were no power tools for building sets. Some sets were constructed of chicken wire and mud. The "steel bars" of the prison cells were made by sanding down pieces of scrap wood because it was cheaper to pay labor than buy round rods of wood. Five hundred Chinese workmen built all the sets from scratch. Even so, the confusion wasn't a total loss. "In the end, it was all worth it," Clouse later said, according to Bruce Thomas's *Fighting Spirit*. "You couldn't have created that Oriental atmosphere in Hollywood for a million dollars."

Early on, Lee walked off the set after an argument with Raymond Chow, whom he thought was trying to control too much of the project. After that day, there were daily fights between the two. Later, Lee banned Clouse from the set when he was filming the fight scenes. Much to Lee's annoyance, Clouse—who knew nothing about directing action—tried to get his fingers in the scenes. If Clouse was there, Lee wouldn't show up.

Two weeks of shooting passed and still there was nothing of Lee on film. When he finally got in front of the camera, a new problem popped up. He developed a nervous twitch on his face that could easily be seen in close-ups. This problem wasn't too surprising—Lee was under a tremendous amount of psychological pressure. *Enter the Dragon* was the big chance he had waited his whole life for. It meant nothing if he couldn't pull it off. Thankfully, his twitch was short-lived. In the morning, the crew managed to ad-lib with long shots and different angles. After lunch, the twitch disappeared.

On top of all the emotional stress, *Enter the Dragon* made enormous demands on Lee's physical energy. In just one take, he might fight 10 to 12 attackers, leaping from side to side, spinning, striking, kicking, and blocking—all with perfect accuracy. The scenes had to be filmed over and over again until they were

Enter the Dragon became the most important movie in Bruce Lee's career. Although there was tension on the set between Lee and director Robert Clouse, *Enter the Dragon* was a certifiable hit and it made Bruce Lee a star in both the United States and Asia.

totally convincing. Sometimes, it took 15 to 20 takes, often in the intense heat and humidity. Lee didn't have a stunt double to give him a rest. After all, who could match his abilities? Still, even after a long day of filming, Lee often went straight to his exercise room to work out and experiment with new techniques. He became restless at night. Unable to sleep, he'd sit up working out fight scenes and drawing diagrams of the action. Before long, his skin paled, and he started to look ill.

The final scenes of the movie were shot in a hurry, as the dungeon scenery cracked and crumbled. Despite all the glitches, the dungeon fight ranks as another one of Lee's most stunning sequences ever filmed. Lee anticipated *Enter the Dragon* would be his biggest movie yet, but it also took the biggest toll on him.

BRUSH WITH DEATH

On May 10, 1973, Lee sat in a tiny dubbing room at Golden Harvest studio, looping dialogue for *Enter the Dragon*. He recorded his voice over a loop of film until the new voice matched the original lip movements as closely as possible. In order to achieve complete silence, the air-conditioning had been shut down, and the room was sweltering. Lee was still exhausted from the grueling weeks of filming. He casually commented that he felt a little faint and needed to step out for a minute. He walked to the bathroom and splashed his face with cold water. Suddenly, his legs gave out, and he collapsed.

The next thing he remembered was the sound of footsteps approaching. As he started to come to, he fingered around on the floor, pretending he had dropped his glasses. Twenty minutes had passed since Lee had left the dubbing room, and the assistant could see that something was wrong. Lee was drenched with sweat and couldn't walk on his own. Suddenly, Lee dropped again. His body writhed, and he was seized by a fit of vomiting and struggled to breathe.

Friends rushed Lee to a nearby hospital. He was running a fever of 105 degrees. Several times, he opened his eyes for just a moment. Then, they would roll back as he lost consciousness. All the while, he gasped for each breath as if it was his last. He later admitted he felt very close to death. "I'm going to fight it," he told himself, according to *The Bruce Lee Story*. "I'm not going to give up." Somehow he knew if he thought anything else he would certainly die. The doctors immediately hooked Lee up to a respirator and slid a breathing tube down his throat. They then started an intravenous glucose drip, while they tried to figure out what was wrong. At first, they suggested exhaustion, kidney failure, or epilepsy. Upon examination, they discovered a swelling of fluid pressing on his brain. They diagnosed Lee with cerebral edema.

No longer conscious, Lee was given Manitol, a dehydrating agent, to reduce the swelling. Lee suddenly became agitated and started having seizure-like convulsions. Doctors had to tape down his arms and legs so he wouldn't hurt himself. Even four doctors had trouble holding him steady while they secured the tape. An ambulance then took him to St. Theresa's. If he showed no improvement, the doctors were ready to perform brain surgery. Luckily, as the days passed he seemed to come out of it.

When he had recovered enough to travel, he and Linda flew back to Los Angeles. A team at the University of California Medical Center came to the same conclusion as the doctors in Hong Kong—excess fluid around the brain. The doctors prescribed Dilantin, a drug used to calm brain activity in epilepsy patients. Still, the whole incident had the doctors bewildered. Lee's body was in such superb condition.

Lee and Linda checked into the Beverly Hills Hotel for a week. Actor and friend Bob Wall visited Lee several times that week and noticed how miserable he looked. "He looked chalky white and thin, nervous and upset," he recalled in *Fighting Spirit*. "I tried to get him to join me in training but he didn't go out running once in that whole week. That just wasn't Bruce Lee." Lee's once confident, bold personality turned to anxious, unsure, and worn out. His collapse had really scared him. Occasionally, he'd talk as if he was going to die. But when friends advised him to take a few months off, Lee refused. He insisted he had to promote the film. He'd worked so hard to get where he was. He wasn't about to let it slip away.

While he was in Los Angeles, Lee finished up the final lines of dialogue for *Enter the Dragon*. At an early screening of the film at Warner Brothers, Lee watched the screen with anticipation and scrutiny. When the lights came back on, according to *Fighting Spirit*, he punched the air and exclaimed, "This is the one!" Warner executives agreed it was a winner and scheduled the premiere at Graumann's Chinese Theater in Hollywood on August 24. Bruce also planned to appear on several TV shows to promote the film, including the *Johnny Carson Show* in New York. Lee had high hopes for *Enter the Dragon* and predicted it would gross $20 million in the United States. "This is the movie I'm proud of," he stated, according to *The Celebrated Life of the Golden Dragon*, "because it has been made for the U.S. audience as well as for the European and Oriental. . . . This is definitely the biggest movie I ever made. I'm excited to see what will happen."

As soon as other filmmakers got wind of *Enter the Dragon*, Lee got flooded with offers. Suddenly, every studio in the world had the perfect movie for Bruce Lee. Warner Brothers, too, threw a hefty offer on the table, five more features paying $150,000 per film. Lee had achieved his ultimate goal—he was the biggest Chinese star in the world.

FAREWELL TO THE LITTLE DRAGON

Around noon on July 20, 1973, Lee sat in his study, hunched over books and papers sprawled out on his desk. Linda interrupted to let him know she was going out to lunch with a girlfriend. Lee told her that Raymond Chow was coming over that afternoon to talk about script ideas for *The Game of Death*. He also mentioned they would probably go out to dinner later that evening. Chow arrived around 2:00 in the afternoon and stayed until about 4:00. Afterward, Lee drove to the home of actress Betty Ting-pei, who he hoped would play a leading role in his new film. Lee and Betty went over the script together. A while later, Lee complained of a headache, and Betty fetched him an Equagesic tablet, a kind of super aspirin her doctor had prescribed.

Around 7:30 that evening, Lee complained he wasn't feeling well. He asked Betty if he could lie down in the bedroom for a while. When it was time to meet Chow for dinner, Betty tried to wake Lee from his nap, but he wouldn't get up. Finally, Chow telephoned Betty to find out why they were late. She told him she couldn't wake Bruce. Immediately, Chow rushed to her apartment.

As far as Chow could tell, Lee was sleeping peacefully and nothing seemed out of the ordinary. When he too was unable to wake Lee, he ordered Betty to call a doctor. The doctor spent ten minutes trying to revive Lee before he called for an ambulance, which rushed Lee to Queen Elizabeth Hospital. On his way out the door, Chow called Linda.

"Would you go to the Queen Elizabeth Hospital right away?" he asked Linda in a tone of urgency, as she recounted in *The Bruce Lee Story*. "Bruce is on his way there—in an ambulance."

"What happened?" Linda demanded.

"I don't know—something like last time," Chow said.

Instantly alarmed, Linda darted out the door. She arrived at the hospital 15 minutes before the ambulance. When she asked the man at the desk if Lee was there, he responded, "Somebody must be joking—we don't know anything about it." For a moment, Linda wondered if it was just some sort of wild rumor. There had been headlines in Hong Kong newspapers before claiming Bruce was dead. Perhaps this was just another mistake. Linda was about to call home when a mess of paramedics burst into the emergency ward. They were all huddled over Lee, who was lying on a stretcher. One doctor was frantically pounding his chest, trying to keep his heart beating.

A minute later, the doctors sped Lee down a corridor to an intensive-care unit. There, they injected a stimulant into his heart and shocked him with electric paddles. A nurse tried to pull Linda away, saying, "I don't think you want to see this." But Linda struggled free and insisted, "Leave me alone—I want to know what's happening." About this time, Linda noticed that Lee was hooked up to an EKG machine that was recording his heartbeat. It was showing a flat line. Bruce Lee was dead. Linda just couldn't believe that a man with so much vitality and inner force could die. She refused to use the word dead to describe Lee. Instead, she asked the doctor, "Is he alive?" The doctor solemnly shook his head.

Five days later, 30,000 mourners gathered on Maple Street outside the Kowloon Funeral Parlour. People filled the street, crowded balconies, and even lined the rooftops to catch a glimpse of the kung fu idol. It was the largest funeral Hong Kong ever witnessed.

Inside, Lee's body lay in an open bronze casket. The air in the funeral home was thick with the smell of burning candles, incense, and fresh-cut flowers. Linda buried her face in the folds of her traditional mourning clothes—a white robe and head-dress. She hid her blood-shot eyes behind dark sunglasses. At the start of the ceremony, the casket was not present, just a picture of Lee on an altar. Above the photograph hung a banner that read "A Star Sinks in the Sea of Art." Linda, Brandon, and Shannon sat on cushions on the floor. After a while, the Chinese band played a traditional funeral song as the casket was wheeled up to the altar. One by one, mourners filed past the coffin to say farewell to the Little Dragon. Long after the funeral was over, police still patrolled the streets, urging people to go home.

Lee had two funeral ceremonies—one in Hong Kong and one in Seattle, where he was buried. The second service was more private than the first. Lee was buried in the Chinese outfit he wore in *Enter the Dragon*. He often wore it around the house because he thought it was comfortable. Linda decided to bury

At age 32, Bruce Lee died of cerebral edema on July 20, 1973, in the home of actress Betty Ting Pei. In the photograph above, garlands and wreaths surround Lee's casket, which was buried at the Lake View Cemetery in Seattle, Washington. Although Lee's cause of death is listed as death by misadventure on his death certificate, there have been many conspiracy theories floating around stating different reasons for his untimely passing.

her husband in Seattle, where the light rain he loved to walk in falls often. "I think his happiest times were spent in Seattle," Linda explained in *The Bruce Lee Story*. At the grave site, Linda quoted Lee's words on death. "The soul of a man is an embryo in the body of man," Lee once said. "The day of death is the day of awakening. The spirit lives on." James Coburn spoke the last words, "Farewell, brother. It has been an honor to share this space in time with you. As a friend and as a teacher, you have given to me, have brought my physical, spiritual and psychological selves together. Thank you. May peace be with you." He then dropped his white pallbearer gloves into the open grave. No doubt, those attending the funeral wanted to quote Lee's line from *Fists of Fury*: "How can a healthy man die?"

LEGACY

Unfortunately, the drama that surrounded Lee's life did not end with his death. The press went wild with theories about his sudden passing. Some people claimed Lee had been murdered by traditional kung fu masters who hated his non-classical style and his openness with Westerners. A few even went as far as accusing Run Run Shaw or even Raymond Chow. They, too, probably had trouble believing a healthy man could just keel over and die. Others suggested he was a drug addict who died of some sort of overdose because slight traces of marijuana were found in his stomach. Perhaps it was a reaction to the potent Equagesic Betty had given him. Or quite possibly, his death stemmed from his previous brain swelling condition. Even more likely, it was a combination of both.

After Lee's death, numerous autopsies were performed. One of the doctors at Queen Elizabeth examined his skull. Although the doctor found no injuries, Lee's brain was "swollen like a sponge," weighing 1,575 grams compared to the normal 1,400 grams, according to Linda's book, *The Bruce Lee Story*. But he did not die of a brain hemorrhage because none of the blood vessels were blocked or broken. When foul play and drug overdose were ruled out, reporters asked Linda if she was relieved. She flatly replied, "Well, it doesn't really change anything, does it?"

Lee was not present for his big premiere, but his inklings were right. *Enter the Dragon* was a phenomenal success. Since its release, the film has grossed more than $200 million in the United States. Although *Game of Death* was incomplete at the time of his death, it was "finished" and released posthumously in 1978. Eventually, Lee's first three films were also released in the United States. *The Big Boss* was retitled *Fists of Fury*, and *Fist of Fury* became *The Chinese Connection*. *Way of the Dragon* was also rereleased as *Return of the Dragon*. Since his death, no other martial artist has come close to Lee's almost supernatural powers.

CHRONOLOGY

1940 *November 27* Bruce Lee is born in the hour of the dragon (between 6:00 and 8:00 in the morning) in the year of the dragon. His parents name him Jun Fan "return again" Li.

1941 *February* Lee appears in his first film at three months old.

1941 Lee moves to Hong Kong with his parents.

TIMELINE

November 27, 1940
Bruce Lee is born in the hour of the dragon in the year of the dragon.

1953
Lee begins studying kung fu under Yip Man of the wing chun system.

1964
Lee performs at the International Karate Tournament in Long Beach, California; Lee marries Linda Emery on August 17.

1940 — 1964

February 1941
Lee appears in his first film at three months old.

Lee moves to Hong Kong with his parents.

April 29, 1959
Lee leaves Hong Kong for the United States and arrives on May 17.

1946 Lee begins filming his first Cantonese film. He stars in 18 films by age 18.

1952 Lee enters La Salle College, a Catholic boys' school.

1953 Lee begins studying kung fu under Yip Man of the wing chun system.

1958 Lee wins the Crown Colony Cha-Cha Championship; he enters Saint Francis Xavier on March 29.

1959 *April 29* Lee leaves Hong Kong for the United States and arrives on May 17; on September 3, he moves in with Ruby Chow and

1972
Lee films a second movie for Golden Harvest called *Fist of Fury.*

Lee makes his debut as a director and actor in *Way of the Dragon.*

1966
Shooting for *The Green Hornet* series begins.

1965

1973

1965
Brandon Bruce Lee is born on February 1.

1971
Lee films *The Big Boss* in Thailand.

1973
Lee starts *Enter the Dragon.*

Lee dies from brain swelling.

enrolls at Edison Technical School in Seattle, Washington.

1960 *December 2* Lee graduates from Edison.

1961 *May 27* Lee begins college at the University of Washington.

1963 Lee returns home to Hong Kong to visit his family from March to August; he opens the Jun Fan Gung Fu Institute in Seattle in October.

1964 Lee quits the University in May; he leaves Seattle to establish another Gung Fu Institute in Oakland, California; he performs at the International Karate Tournament in Long Beach, California; Lee marries Linda Emery on August 17.

1965 Brandon Bruce Lee is born on February 1; Lee had his first screen test three days later; Hoi Cheun, Lee's father, dies on February 8.

1966 The Lees move to Los Angeles in March; shooting for *The Green Hornet* series begins on June 6; Lee plays Kato—the Green Hornet's sidekick.

1967 Lee opens the Los Angeles branch of the Jun Fan Gung Fu Institute in February; he is asked to appear in one episode of the *Ironside* TV series.

1968 Lee works as the technical director of *The Wrecking Crew* in July; the Lees move to Bel Air on October 1.

1969 Shannon Emery Lee is born on April 19.

1970 Lee begins working with screenwriter Stirling Silliphant on his martial arts film *The Silent Flute*.

1971 Lee films the first episode of TV series *Longstreet* in June; he begins developing a TV series for Warner Brothers called *The Warrior* and finds out later he will not star in it; Lee films *The Big Boss* in Thailand for Golden Harvest Studios; the movie breaks all previous box-office records in Hong Kong.

1972 He films a second movie for Golden Harvest called *Fist of Fury*; again, the film breaks all Hong Kong records set by his previous film; Lee makes his debut as a director and actor in *Way of the Dragon,* which he also wrote; this film again shatters all records in Hong Kong; Lee begins filming his next film, *Game of Death* in October.

1973 Lee interrupts filming *Game of Death* to start a feature film for Warner Brothers titled *Enter the Dragon;* this role is his first lead role in a U.S. film; on May 10, Lee collapses at Golden Harvest while dubbing for *Enter the Dragon;* doctors diagnose him with cerebral edema; Lee dies from his brain swelling and a reaction to a prescription medication on July 20; he is buried in Lakeview Cemetery in Seattle on July 31.

GLOSSARY

archetypal—Original or symbolic.

bil jee jab—Thrusting fingers, a move in wing chun that can deliver a devastating blow.

central axis—The area around the waist of an opponent's body.

chi sao (sticking hands)—Not an actual fighting move, rather, an awareness to the shifting balance of physical forces during a fight.

contact reflex—An ability to "fee" any more or any intended move, even before it is made.

jeet kune do—Bruce Lee's style of kung fu; a philosophy of oneness with nature and experiencing the harmony of yin and yang; there are three stages to the jeet kune do philosophy: the Primitive Stage, ruled by automatic reactions and responses; the Stage of Art, which takes place when training in kung fu and gaining the knowledge of combat; and the Stage of Alertness, when a student can use the knowledge of combat to react at an unconscious level.

judo—A Japanese form of wrestling in which an opponents weight and strength are used against him or her.

karate—A Japanese style of self-defense, using sharp, quick blows with the hands and feet.

kung fu (gung fu)—Originally a term that meant "the accomplishment of a difficult task," today refers to many styles of the Chinese martial arts; according to martial art folklore, the creator of kung fu was an early-sixteenth-century Indian monk named Bodhidharma.

kwoon—Chinese word for school.

martial arts—Styles of self-defense, such as karate and kung fu, that originated in the East or Asia.

meditate—To relax the body and mind, release the body and mind into a state that transcends consciousness.

occupation—A time when a foreign country rules another country, usually with a military presence and sometimes with cruel oppression.

opium—A narcotic drug found in certain poppy seeds with a painkiller-like affect.

oppression—Being ruled under a cruel and unjust authority.

t'ai chi—A slow, soft style of martial arts, often used as therapy to promote health and longevity.

Taoism—A Chinese religion and philosophy that stresses simplicity and selflessness.

tarot cards—Cards with pictures and symbols used to predict the future.

wing chun—A condensed form of kung fu, designed to deliver the maximum amount of anguish with a minimal amount of movement.

yang—One of two forces at play in the universe, represents the masculine active force, such as heat, light, sound and infinity.

yin—The other of the two forces at play in the universe, represents the feminine or passive force, such as coldness, darkness, stillness, and the finite.

BIBLIOGRAPHY/ FURTHER READING

Campbell, Sid, and Greglon Yimm Lee. *The Dragon and the Tiger: Volume 2, the Oakland Years*. Berkeley, Calif.: Frog, Ltd., 2005.

Lee, Bruce. *Jeet Kune Do*. Boston: Tuttle Publishing, 1997.

Lee, Bruce. *Striking Thoughts: Bruce Lee's Wisdom for Daily Living*. Boston: Tuttle Publishing, 2000.

Lee, Bruce. *The Tao of Gung Fu*. Boston: Tuttle Publishing, 1997.

Lee, Bruce, and John Little, ed. *Bruce Lee: Artist of Life*. Boston: Tuttle Publishing, 1999.

Lee, Bruce, and John Little, ed. *Bruce Lee: The Celebrated Life of the Golden Dragon*. Boston: Tuttle Publishing, 2000.

Lee, Bruce, and John Little, ed. *Letters of the Dragon: Correspondence, 1958–1973*. Boston: Tuttle Publishing, 1998.

Lee, Linda. *The Bruce Lee Story*. Santa Clarita, Calif.: Ohara Publications, 1989.

Little, John A. *Bruce Lee: A Warrior's Journey*. New York: Contemporary Books, 2001.

Thomas, Bruce. *Bruce Lee: Fighting Spirit*. Berkeley, Calif.: Frog, Ltd., 1994.

Uyehara, M. *Bruce Lee: The Incomparable Fighter*. Santa Clarita, Calif.: Ohara Publications, 1988.

INDEX

ABOUT
THE AUTHOR

RACHEL A. KOESTLER-GRACK has written and edited nonfiction books since 1999. During her career, she has worked extensively with historical topics, ranging from the Middle Ages to the colonial era to the civil rights movement. In addition, she has written numerous biographies on a variety of historical and contemporary figures. Rachel lives with her husband and daughter on a hobby farm near Glencoe, Minnesota.

PHOTO
CREDITS